Teaching
Biblical Faith

Other Abingdon Press Books by Jack L. Seymour

Teaching the Way of Jesus
A Deacon's Heart
Mapping Christian Education
Educating Christians
Theological Approaches to Christian Education
Contemporary Approaches to Christian Education

Teaching
Biblical Faith

Leading Small Group
Bible Studies

Jack L. Seymour

Abingdon Press
Nashville

TEACHING BIBLICAL FAITH:
LEADING SMALL GROUP BIBLE STUDIES

Copyright © 2015 by Abingdon Press

This book is printed on acid-free paper.

Library of Congress Cataloging-in-Publication Data

Seymour, Jack L. (Jack Lee), 1948–
    Teaching biblical faith : leading small group Bible studies / Jack L. Seymour. — First
[edition].
    pages cm
    ISBN 978-1-63088-430-7 (binding: soft back) 1. Bible—Hermeneutics. 2. Bible—
Study and teaching. 3. Church group work. 4. Christian education—Philosophy. I. Title.
    BS476.S49 2015
    220.071—dc23

                                                                    2015008530

15 16 17 18 19 20 21 22 23 24—10 9 8 7 6 5 4 3 2 1

MANUFACTURED IN THE UNITED STATES OF AMERICA

For those faithful believers who study the Bible to grow in faith and vocation—to connect their lives to God's dreams for the world

Contents

Contents

Part Three: Advice for Teachers and Leaders

Preface

This book is about "best practices" in biblical study. Several proven strategies for biblical teaching are described in short chapters. All have been tested. They empower believers to grow in faith and discipleship. While each can be used for personal devotion and study, they are best used in small groups where friends hold each other accountable for growth in an atmosphere of support, care, and commitment.

The thesis of this book is that Christian living is "biblical living"—a process of seeking to understand and live God's grace and call in light of the witness of our forebears. For Christians, the books of the Bible are our source. These books gained authority in the early church and have continued to have authority because of the authenticity of their witness, shaping Christian living for almost two thousand years.

Through the Bible, we encounter directly the "way of Jesus" and the ways that followers sought to be faithful to his message of redemptive community. In turn, we each seek to live redemptively in our day. Doing so requires ongoing study, support, and reflection. Study shapes our identity and calls us to vocation as we seek to be faithful.

Biblical living cannot be fully understood without knowledge of and interaction with our Jewish brothers and sisters and their use of scripture. Jesus was socialized in the Jewish community of Galilee. The God to whom he witnessed was known through that world. Moreover, he learned the meanings of scripture, the reality of being children of God, and efforts to embody God's grace, redemption, and justice in that milieu and cultural situation.

The following approaches have been tested in congregations and seminary classrooms. For over twenty-five years I have shared in teaching a course at Garrett-Evangelical Theological Seminary, Teaching for Biblical Faith. Together with our students (lay and clergy) and their congregations, we teachers have explored approaches to biblical living and biblical study. They have been taught in congregations and public settings. Of course, particular individuals and congregations have found some to be more effective and easier to teach. I invite you to use these best practices. Use the ones that empower your study and living. Join in the journey to teach and learn as faithful witnesses of biblical faith.

I thank those laity and students who shared their learnings and who tested approaches in congregations. They have taught me much. I thank friends at First United Methodist Church in Evanston who have journeyed in faith with me. I thank David Teel and Paul Franklyn of Abingdon Press, who are committed to enhancing Bible study among the people of God. I particularly thank my colleagues at Garrett-Evangelical Theological Seminary who cotaught classes with me. Their imprint is clearly present in this book: Reginald Blount, Margaret Ann Crain, Virginia Lee, and Linda Vogel. Above all, I thank my life partner, Margaret Ann Crain. We have taught, written, and built a life together. Her service to seminary, annual conference, denomination, and the wider church is an example of seeking to live biblical faith.

This book is dedicated to our grandchildren, whose parents share deep and important values with them and offer them goals for living that indeed make a difference.

Introduction: Bible Study Matters

"Let's help the children know the Bible. They know a few stories, but not how to connect them. They don't have a sense of the whole."

That is how our planning began. The education committee decided to provide a set of key biblical stories on which the children and youth could draw. We wanted them to have a sense of the whole—the interconnections. After conversations with parents, Sunday school teachers, our pastors, and educators from neighboring churches, we developed a set of Old Testament stories that we would teach the next fall in all of the classes for children and youth. We knew it would be a lot of work. We hoped it would be worth it.

We met many times, negotiated, and decided on ten key stories (texts):

- creation

- call of Sarah and Abraham

- freedom from Egypt (Passover)

- wandering in the wilderness, finding the promised land

- great leaders: Saul, David, and Solomon

- Ruth and Naomi

- Job

- great prophets, the call for justice

- fall of Jerusalem and captivity in Babylon

- restoring the temple and the Second Temple (here we stretched the Old Testament and connected to the New)

We gathered resources—from the scripture, art, historical studies, and storybooks. We recruited teachers and promised them three two-hour teacher workshops where we would teach them the texts and their background, and provide help in developing lessons. Third, we looked to September, sending reminders to all the parents, children, and youth. In addition, we met with our pastor to plan connections between the stories taught and her sermons. We advertised both in and outside the church. We ran errands for teachers.

It was an amazing fall! Teachers exuded confidence, intimately knowing their texts. They passionately entered into learning with the students, proclaiming that teaching itself caused them to have a richer understanding and a hunger to learn more. A couple even asked what were the next ten stories they needed to know to understand the Hebrew Bible more fully—Torah, Prophets, and Writings? They wanted more study.

Then there was a miracle we had not planned. Parents saw a confidence in their children, noting their joy in Sunday school. Attendance remained high—higher than at any time in recorded congregational wisdom. As children told parents what they were learning, parents began to both worry and hunger. Worry—their children were fast passing their own knowledge of the Bible, and in one ten-week series! Parents told us that they had a vague knowledge of the biblical story, knowing about Noah, Ruth, and Joseph. But they wondered: What really was the big deal about Moses's birth, why did the Hebrew nation wander in the desert, how do the words of the prophets relate to today, and what really is expected of us? What does God's faithfulness and justice mean? Hunger—yes, the parents hungered for a sense of the whole and for knowledge in how to use these traditions to make decisions in their everyday living.

Parents asked us for help. Could we repeat this study? An opportunity. After conversation and some "market research," we began the next fall with ten New Testament stories taught to all of the classes in the church—even initiating some new small groups in new times and locations. We repeated the process of planning, coordinated preaching and teaching, prepared resources for teachers, created a devotional book parallel to the stories, and provided support for all who taught.

It worked! The ten New Testament stories were received with excitement. The following year we repeated the Old Testament stories. And then the next year, we focused on ten historical stories that changed the church. We had surveyed key moments in the Bible and in the historical development of the church and its beliefs and practices. In addition, in the spring of each year, we offered classes in how to use this knowledge to make sense of the world and to live faithfully. Without a doubt, the church's education was enhanced.

Of course, a lot of our success was simply that we did something new with excitement; nevertheless we satisfied a worry and a hunger of the congregation in how to energize faith with directed and sequenced study. Adults reported that they were able to draw on biblical and historical stories in conversations with others. They thought about their learnings as they made decisions.

People became more biblically literate. Moreover, the teachers were joyous, telling us how their searching of the scriptures enriched their lives. They were passionate advocates: study transforms living! We all witnessed it. Above all else, we were able to have conversations about the meaning of our faiths—in a fair and open manner, respecting differences and connecting our faith to our Jewish and Christian heritages.

In fact, small group study helped us consider faithfulness as we made decisions for the church and its partnership with others in the community. The result was that we joined a community ministry with a synagogue and a church. The congregation's experience of study and learning offered confidence, hope, insights, and new life. It tapped a worry and a hunger. People made faith-filled decisions.

Bible to Life; Life to Bible

Church teachers have wondered: Do we begin teaching with Bible or life? Do we make sure people know the biblical story and seek to live it, or do we explore the questions of our lives and see how our faith helps us address them? Common sense offers an answer: Why not both—Bible and experience? We live in a world where few have solid biblical knowledge and few seem able to connect biblical study with living. Yes, we all know some stories and concepts very well, but do we have a sense of the whole? Are we able to draw on aspects of faith as we move through each day?

The people learned biblical stories and witnessed that this learning helped them as they considered the decisions of their lives.

The people in our story learned biblical stories. They witnessed that this learning helped them as they considered the decisions of their lives. How do we help the people of God know the building blocks of their faith lives? How do we help them practice connecting faith and living?

Through the last several years, Margaret Ann Crain, my spouse, and I have been involved in research with laypeople about the concerns that call them to search their faiths and the scriptures. We have listened deeply to their stories and asked them about how they draw on faith resources in daily living. These faithful people gave us an important gift. They described their efforts at seeking to know themselves as Christians (identity) and seeking to live as faithfully as possible (vocation). Of course, they reported failures and confusion as well as some moments of new life and redemption.

We heard how they drew on their faith commitments. For some, it was a personal experience of loss, illness, challenge, brokenness, or reconciliation. For others, it was a public experience of violence, economic exploitation, environmental degradation, war and peace, or conflict resolution. For still others, it was meeting someone of a different faith and seeing how he or she lived.[1]

People seem to follow a regular pattern in making sense of and discovering meaning in these situations. The steps include

- clarifying and considering an issue or concern;

- critically exploring the content of the biblical and theological tradition;

- engaging in dialogue with oneself, others, and the tradition;

- discerning a considered decision;

- acting on the decision; and

- continuing to reflect on and test the decision and its adequacy.[2]

The people we interviewed told us that they moved through this process regularly. When they struggled with important personal and faith decisions, they appreciated the scriptures that empowered them. They appreciated friends who stood by them. They appreciated groups where they could be open, be vulnerable, and explore.

These steps describe what all of us do. We consider the questions of our lives and the decisions facing us, we explore all of the resources we have, including important faith resources, and we make decisions. This occurs over and over, from mundane moments of deciding on a color to paint our kitchens to the most momentous decisions of our lives about taking a job, caring for a relative, or embarking on a new vocation. In important decisions, our faith plays a crucial role. Bible and life come together.

When we study the biblical texts and explore our lives, we are called to new ways of living, to our deepest hopes and convictions. When we decide, we draw on all the resources we have from friends, work colleagues, and religious institutions. Living is a process of considering the questions and concerns from our everyday, in relationship to exploring our commitments and all of the resources of our faiths, in order to make decisions that are whole, caring, and life giving.[3]

Biblical study matters because it both enhances our knowledge of the resources of our faith and offers a setting where we can ask questions about living faithfully.

Biblical study matters because it both enhances our knowledge of the resources of our faith and offers a setting where we can ask questions about living faithfully. Through biblical study, we ask questions of both the text and our lives. Teaching assists persons in expanding biblical awareness and in practicing the connecting of faith to living.

What to Expect as You Read This Book

Through the chapters of this book, you will be empowered to grow and live as faithful people, embodying biblical faith. Ten approaches to biblical study are shared. We will learn questions to ask of the text and of our lives. The hope is that Bible and living connect, so that amidst life-changing and life-giving moments, we can draw deeply on all the resources at hand.

This book provides "best practices" to Bible study and teaching in the congregation, in homes and communities, and in personal devotion. Some of these ten approaches to biblical study have emerged from scholarship, some from devotional traditions, and some from the global church. Yet, they have all been lived and tested in congregations. They have advantages and disadvantages. You will want to experiment to see which approaches best help you grow, but you'll also want to stretch yourself and see which challenge you to new life.

I promise that when you teach these in a community of care that you will grow in your knowledge of the faith. You will grow in your ability to connect faith with life and grow in your awareness of the richness of scripture. You'll grow in your ability to teach. You'll be surprised as you naturally begin to connect biblical meanings with daily events. In fact, you will engage in practical theological reflection for discipleship.

The hope is that you can peruse the book, pick an approach to teaching and learning, and simply try it.

The format of each short chapter is similar. Each begins with an example, moves to a description of the approach, and offers strengths and weaknesses. The hope is that you can peruse the book, pick an approach to teaching and learning, and simply try it. In a group, you will want to take turns teaching.

Following the chapters about approaches, concrete suggestions are offered to enhance teaching in the congregation. The book then closes with a select bibliography of key books for a congregation's library.

The congregation whose story we told began by teaching a set of stories from the Hebrew Bible to children. It expanded to whole congregation studies with the biblical witness. People reported that they grew in their knowledge of the faith, they began to make connections, and they had resources of faith at hand as they moved through the events of the day. May this study assist you to live faithfully!

PART ONE

Biblical Living and Teaching

Chapter One

Biblical Faith

How do we live as faithful persons? Every day we encounter many beliefs and many perspectives. Advertisements define our wants and needs. Too often we make decisions on the spur of the moment without considering implications—we are caught in the routine. In addition to the differing beliefs of many faiths, we hear great diversity among those who call themselves *Christian*. We often quake when the media names comments as *Christian*—they always highlight the extreme.

Living faithfully takes practice— seeking through prayer, study, community, and service the meanings of Christian living today.

Living faithfully takes practice—seeking through prayer, study, community, and service the meanings of Christian living today.[1] The followers of Jesus found themselves confronting the military power of Rome with its technological superiority. Yes, Rome had improved roads, provided clean water in many places and even sewerage systems, yet at what cost? Romans demanded allegiance. The people they conquered were required to worship their emperors as gods incarnate. Our Jewish forebears resisted these expectations, seeing them as idolatrous—substituting an empire for the God of creation. This resistance was at the heart of Jesus's message. It further empowered the disciples, Paul, and early missionaries to spread the gospel of a hope and new life. They proclaimed how to live in the light of the one, holy God, instead of Caesar.

Just like our forebears whose lives were defined by Roman expectations and hierarchies, our lives are too are often defined simply by our culture's expectations and hierarchies. We lose awareness of what it means to be "children of God," what it means that God has created and is creating, and that God has dreams for a future defined by "shalom"—healing, hope, justice, and community. We also lose awareness that God expects us to be part of that dream—following God's realm (God's kingdom) as agents of shalom.

Seeking Faithfulness

To reclaim our identity as children of God and our vocation as partners in creating, we have to probe the wisdom of our traditions. In prayer and humility, we make decisions about how we will live and act, knowing God is alive in our world.

The Methodist movement initiated by John Wesley had at its core small groups where faithful persons joined together in means of grace—that is, in acts of piety and mercy, like scripture reading, common study, prayer, communion, service, and attendance at worship—to inspire each other for Christian living. These groups often asked members, "How is it with your soul?" How are you living your faith journey? People shared their lives, prayed together, studied together, and supported each other to live holy ways. Lives were changed.

Yet, what does living biblical faith mean? The Bible consists of many books written across time to many different situations with differing understandings and commitments. Jeremiah writes about the events that lead to the people's captivity in Babylon. Ruth deals with issues of inclusion of strangers in God's love and care. Psalms provides prayers and hymns for private and public occasions of worship and petition to God.

In fact, the Bible is a library of books, some from the early Jewish community and others added by the Christian community. The Jewish community eventually organized their books into Torah, Prophets, and Writings. To this, Christians added Gospels and the Letters.

In Jesus's day, both a Torah reading and a prophetic reading (Law and Prophets) were shared at each Sabbath celebration. Studying the books of Torah and Prophets as well as drawing on the wisdom of the Writings was a way of seeking to understand God's gifts and expectations. In fact, the witness of the Jewish synagogues in the diaspora of the Roman Empire was so strong that many Gentiles would gather to listen to their study of scripture. These "God fearers" experienced integrity, hope, and new life—things too often missing in Roman culture.

Jesus and his disciples practiced the traditions of studying and interpreting the Torah and the prophets (see Luke 4, for example). The followers of Jesus continued these practices of reading and studying the scriptures of Law and Prophets.

They later supplemented them with letters from Christian leaders and biographies (gospels) of the life of Jesus. As the communities following Jesus read these texts, they experienced their authenticity to build community and to communicate faithfulness. The books became their "rule" or "measuring stick" (the Greek word *canon*). Studying the scriptures provided directions for living the faith.

Understanding Biblical Faiths

Biblical scholar Walter Brueggemann helps us identify aspects of biblical faith. He sees three faith perspectives in the

Hebrew canon that also affect New Testament understandings. While complementary, each of these faith patterns represents particular commitments and embodies a distinctive form of education. The three are *priestly faith*, the honoring of Torah, tradition, and identity; *prophetic faith*, addressing human and social distress; and *wisdom faith*, seeking to connect the faith to everyday, ordinary events.[2]

Priestly faith seeks to pass on and preserve the traditions of a community. The focus of priestly faith is to clarify what God expects of us. Integrity is found in honoring the faithful witnesses who came before and who shaped the identity of the community. Just like my family sought to teach me what being a "Seymour" meant (identity), priestly faith shaped identity. Teaching thus sought to instruct the people in the expectations and "normative claims of the community."[3]

While respecting the past, *prophetic faith* immerses the believer in the depths of people's pain and the search for God's hope. The great prophets like Hosea, Jeremiah, and Amos called the community to faithfulness. For them, simply following the marks of identity was not sufficient when it did not take into account those on the edge of the community—widows, orphans, and strangers.

In fact, Amos proclaimed God's word: "I hate, I reject your festivals; I don't enjoy your joyous assemblies" (Amos 5:21). Why would God hate what the tradition expected? Because, as Amos said, "Doom to you who turn justice into poison, and throw righteousness to the ground" (5:7); "You crush the weak" and turn away "the poor who seek help" (5:11-12). In other words, prophetic faith is focused on living justice in a particular time and place (vocation). As Amos concludes, "But let justice roll down like waters, and righteousness like an ever-flowing stream" (5:24). Prophetic faith is an alternative imagination focusing on God's ongoing call to faithfulness. Education thus attends to living a vocation of justice.

Finally, the tradition does not have answers for all of life's questions. As new questions and new times arise, *wisdom faith* seeks to help us know what to do and be. No clear instructions from the past define all the situations we face in the future, so how is a person to know how to live? The writers of Proverbs, of Job, of Song of Songs, to name a few, sought to answer the questions of living. Through education, they taught people a way to extend the meanings of the Torah and the Prophets into this new day and time. How do we deal with personal suffering, with love, with primary relationships, with children?

Knowing that definitive answers are not available for everything and knowing that we face circumstances never before imagined, wisdom faith calls for prayer, humility, and theological reflection seeking to discern God's will. The answers of the wisdom writers often were more tentative than the expectations of the Torah or the call of the prophets.

Brueggemann argues that these three patterns tend to lead us in different ways, yet all three are present in the biblical witness. *Priestly faith* focuses on the gifts of the past and how we are to live as holy people. *Prophetic faith* focuses on God's justice and how "creation groans" for the fulfillment of God's dreams. *Wisdom faith* asks how we can be faithful in a new day when the world has so radically changed.

What then is biblical faith? Is it following the tradition, seeking God's justice, or enacting the hopes of the faith in new times and new places? Honestly, we can answer, all three. No wonder there are conflicting views among congregations of faithful people. These three are in dynamic tension seeking to be faithful to a living, creating, transforming, and sustaining God.

> What then is biblical faith? It is following the tradition, seeking God's justice, and enacting the hopes of the faith in new times and new places.

Following Jesus

Yet, we all wish for more clarity. Across differences of experiences, surroundings, and faith stories, we struggle for faithfulness. Without time and colleagues with whom to reflect, without prayer and humility, we miss the richness and depth of biblical faiths.

Christians look to Jesus and his followers to help us understand biblical faith. What Jesus asked of his disciples is a foretaste of what Jesus asks of us. Jesus drew on all three faith patterns.

Like his Jewish colleagues, Jesus's identity was rooted in *priestly faith*—in the Torah.[4] The Shema prayer shaped his teaching and living: God is one, God creates life, God is faithful, and God expects us to be faithful. Love God and neighbor. Remember that when Jesus was questioned by the lawyer about the most important commandment, he quoted the Shema: "The most important one is *Israel, listen! Our God is the one Lord, and you must love the Lord your God with all your heart, with all your being, with all your mind, and with all your strength.* The second is this, *You will love your neighbor as yourself.* No other commandment is greater than these" (Mark 12:29-31).[5] In Luke's version of this questioning, Jesus adds the story we call the good Samaritan, helping the legal expert to realize that "the one who demonstrated mercy" was the one who fulfilled God's commandments (Luke 10:37). Here we see Jesus honoring the Torah and focusing it, as a prophet, on justice and mercy.

Furthermore, even his first sermon shows how important *prophetic faith* was for him. That sermon was a commentary on Isaiah 61:1-2. There Jesus defined faithfulness as "setting free the mistreated, and breaking every yoke . . . sharing your bread with the hungry and bringing the homeless poor into your house, covering the naked when you see them" (Isa 58:6-7). Jesus entered the pain of the people. He was particularly fond of Isaiah. Throughout his teaching, Jesus sought to help people fulfill the profound vocation Isaiah had defined for them as God's people: "Hence, I will also appoint you as light to the nations so that my salvation may reach to the end of the earth" (Isa 49:6). The vocation of the people was to live holy lives so that others could experience through them the integrity, creativity, and holiness of God.

Wisdom faith also claimed Jesus as he extended it to a new day and time—one of oppression and loss. He pointed people to "markers" of faithfulness. One place these markers are obvious is in Jesus's discussion with the disciples of John the Baptist (Matt 11:1-14; Luke 7:18-35). John is in prison for challenging Herod. Jesus, in turn, was becoming well-known for his healings and teachings. He probably was also well-known by the disciples of John, being a relative, having been baptized by John, and perhaps even living for a time as a member of John's group. When John's disciples inquire of Jesus, Jesus points to the heart of the redemptive ministry in which he is engaging: "Go, report to John what you have seen and heard. *Those who were blind are able to see.* Those who were crippled now walk. People with skin diseases are cleansed. *Those who were deaf now hear. Those who were dead are raised up. And good news is preached to the poor*" (Luke 7:22). Coupling Luke 4 and 10, the markers to which Jesus points at the heart of his ministry and that of his followers are the following:

- healing the sick,

- giving sight to the blind,

- offering hearing to those who are deaf,

- forgiving those who have sinned,

- proclaiming release to prisoners,

- preaching the good news to the poor, the least of these,

- restoring community, and

- enacting shalom.[6]

For Jesus, then, biblical faith is an activity of discernment. It is living the gifts of the Torah by loving God and neighbor. It is touching the distress of the people with prophetic mercy and justice. Furthermore, it is seeking through practical wisdom to see and live the markers of God's realm—places where redemptive living was present every day.

These markers set directions for his followers who called people to the living God. Such a message challenged Roman society and order. As the followers of Jesus grew, they were not defined by ethnicity, as was the practice in the ancient world. Their actions were unusual: they practiced peace, resisting both worshipping and fighting for the Roman emperor (therefore they were called atheists by Romans for not believing in Roman gods, and they were persecuted); they crossed social boundaries by gathering rich and poor together in sacramental meals; and they shared the gifts of the table—the gifts of God's healing shalom.

It seems complicated: How do we attend to tradition, open ourselves to God's justice for the brokenhearted, and discern our vocation in new times and places? Practices that connect teaching, community reflection, worship, prayer, and discernment help us learn to live faithfully. We enter these processes with humility and openness, yet only with intentional and sustained teaching do we grow in living biblical faiths.

Chapter Two

Teaching Biblical Faith

For Christians, teaching biblical faith thus means teaching so that people know their identity as children of God, are able to live their vocation as agents of God's shalom or peace in the world, and follow Jesus into new times and places. We are formed as we study the meanings of faith and seek to live in mission to the wider world.[1] Small groups of committed persons are essential to our learning. They listen, support, and hold us accountable as we seek to connect faith and living.

Teaching Practices in the Bible

The Bible itself witnesses to a vigorous plan of teaching and learning. People connected their living to their study of scripture. Educational practices emerged in the Jewish tradition to teach identity and vocation. These practices affected Jesus and subsequently were refined in the church. Faith education connected worship, study, prayer, and living.

A first example is the Sabbath itself. The Sabbath was a day of study. Each Sabbath, people celebrated meals of remembrance and hope. *Shabbat* was the day when God's actions were remembered. *Shabbat* was a day of justice when one's entire household was freed to celebrate the life-giving presence of God. Each week the people read from holy texts (Torah and Prophets) and discussed their meanings. Studying the Law and Prophets was the heart of all teaching and learning.

A second example was the yearly festivals where people remembered and reengaged the acts of God. Scripture and living were connected. Look at the three festivals prescribed in scripture (see Deut 16; Exod 23:10-19; and Lev 23:9-14). The Festival of Passover (*Pesach*), in the spring, recognized that God freed the people from Egypt and made them God's people. Freedom then was not simply a moment in the past, but the ongoing way God worked, even in times of persecution. In turn, freedom from oppression was at the heart of Jesus's message as he confronted the powers that destroyed life options for his neighbors in Galilee. He pointed to markers of God's realm even in the midst of oppression. Thus, we are pointed to God's present acts to free people to be and live as children of God.

Seven weeks after Passover, at the end of spring and beginning of summer was the Festival of Weeks (*Shavuot* or Pentecost). During this time, the people remembered that God gave them the Ten Commandments and the Torah to define how they were to live. Jesus in turn reminded the people of the "law" God expected them to fulfill. He called them to love God and neighbor. He interpreted the law in the Sermon on the Mount (Matt 5–7; Luke 6:17-49). Continuing today, these expectations of how we are to serve God and care for each other are at the heart of education.

The third festival was the fall Festival of Booths (*Sukkot*) reminding the people that when they had been freed from Egypt and wandered in the desert that God continued to care for them. They were reminded of their total dependence on God for direction and even for food (manna) and life. Jesus, in turn, reminded the people that God was the one who gave them life and nurtured them (Matt 6:25-34). Faithful living is being connected to God's hopes for life.

Faithful living is being connected to God's hopes for life.

Through reflection on scripture each Sabbath and remembering the great acts of God, the people attended to God's creating, God's forgiveness, and God's call. Here is a rich community education process. The people turned to the holy texts of the Law and the Prophets to define what it meant to be God's people, to be dependent on God, and how they were to live faithfully for God.[2] All of these educational settings involved study—connecting scripture and living.

These very forms of biblical education were extended in the community of Jesus's followers. As the Acts of the Apostles records (2:43-47; 4:32-25), they gathered studying the Law and Prophets, praying together, and sharing in a holy meal. They focused their lives on both the traditions Jesus honored and the ongoing redemptive experiences of following Jesus. The pattern of the Hebrew synagogues of reading scripture and its exposition was connected with their own witnessing of how their lives were being transformed. Together this attention on the past and the present connected them to the journey that Jesus's living, healing, and teaching had launched.

As we know, the earliest Christian writings that became "scriptures" emerged as people sought to understand their lives, teach the power of Jesus's message, and shape emerging communities. For example, Paul's letters were written to teach communities ways to face disagreements. Later, Gospel writers wove stories of Jesus into community issues. Matthew, for example, sought to connect Christian living to the stories and expectations of the Jewish faith. Luke extended the message to Gentile believers. Other letters like those from James and John assisted believers in knowing who they were as God's children (their identity) and how they were to live as God's followers through Jesus (their vocation).

We study to live faithfully.

In fact, communities of followers of Jesus explicitly defined the importance of studying the scriptures: "For teaching, for showing mistakes, for correcting, and for training character, so that the person who belongs to God can be equipped to do everything that is good" (2 Tim 3:16-17). We study to live faithfully!

The scriptures we call the Bible emerged in the dynamic efforts of Jesus's followers to define their identity and vocation—as they taught the meanings of faithfulness. Study and living merged. The books that became the Bible gained authority because they explained to people the new life and the redemptive community they were experiencing.[3] Just as the early followers turned to these traditions to teach them and form character, we too turn to them and study them to be taught and be formed.

Teaching Biblical Faith

The thesis of this book is that to live as faithful people, to embody biblical faith, we need to study the scriptures deeply. We need to use all of the resources at hand to assist us in this process. We need our colleagues in faith to sit and struggle with us. I agree with my Methodist ancestors that it takes all of the "means of grace" to grow in faith—studying scripture, prayer, community conversation and reflection, the sacraments, worship, and acts of mercy and justice.[4] A key means of grace in the Methodist tradition is "Christian conferencing," reflecting together and committing publicly to those who hold us accountable.

To live as faithful people, to embody biblical faith, we need to study the scriptures deeply.

A few weeks ago we were having dinner with good friends. We were looking for another time to get together. One of us suggested Tuesday. Our friend immediately spoke up and said, "Sorry, I can't do Tuesday. That is when my Bible study group is meeting at our condo. I wouldn't miss it for anything."

As we talked more about her experience with the group, we discovered it was a very diverse group, by age and outlook, of seven to twelve people. Some had been active in churches for years and others were new to the church. Even a couple who had been hurt by churches in the past risked attending the Bible study group. Yet, over the two years they had been meeting, they had developed a fellowship of care, study, and service. Each week naturally included stories from their lives. When any felt burdened or hurt, the group was a place to share. Each week included a regular march through a portion of scripture. They had moved from lectionary study, to book study, to topical reflection, and to sharing favorite passages.

They all witnessed how their biblical knowledge had increased. It was cumulative—studying built on studying; ideas connected with other ideas. Of course, they had to miss some weeks, yet the Bible study had become a critical part of their faith growth. In fact, when issues hit their community, they asked what would be the faithful thing for them to do.

Never self-satisfied, they allowed for differences of opinion, respecting the ways their friends lived the faith. The congregation that they attended is a lively community of people of many ages from many backgrounds. Their Bible study group provides a focused setting for study, a set of friends from which to network with others, and a community of care and accountability that indeed asks, "How is it with your soul? How are we together living the faith?"

The task is not to become the definitive experts on scripture. It is to come to know God, to struggle to understand to what God is calling us, and to commit in the presence of others to actions on behalf of faith in God.

We enter into study in community with prayer and respect. The scriptures are a witness by others of another time to how God was active in their lives and how the richness of the Hebrew tradition and the redemptive experiences of the early Christian tradition empower living. As we study in groups, we will not always see eye to eye. We need to keep an attitude of humility and respect. Yet, we can learn to question each other, support each other, and become inspirations for each other.

The task is not to become the definitive experts on scripture. Scripture study is not an end in itself. It is the means witnessed to by countless generations of faithful people to come to know God, to struggle to understand to what God is calling us, and to commit in the presence of others to actions on behalf of faith in God.

Encountering God's dream for living is the goal. How are we seeing the richness of the tradition, how are we living the depth of God's love to the distressed that surround us, and how are we seeking to extend the life-giving presence known in the Jewish and Christian traditions into our present? Or, in other words, how do we join Jesus in seeing and living the markers of the faith to which he witnessed? How do we participate with God in the following?

- healing the sick

- giving sight to the blind

- offering hearing to those who are deaf

- forgiving those who have sinned

- proclaiming release to prisoners

- preaching the good news to the poor, the least of these

- restoring community

- enacting shalom[5]

As you read this book, I invite you to try different approaches and grow in your knowledge of the scriptures and their ability to impact your living of biblical faith. I invite you to join a regular Bible study group. I invite you to make Bible study a part of your ongoing devotion and reading. I invite you to try to teach and learn from these approaches to Bible study. I invite you to seek to live biblical faith.

PART TWO

Basic Approaches to Small Group Bible Study

Chapter Three

Historical (Exegetical) Study

What Did the Biblical Writer Want to Say?

Have you ever read a book and wondered why it was written? As a child, I loved Mary Shelley's *Frankenstein*. As all good boys from the 1950s were, I was enthused by creatures and science. It was the era of television. I was amazed as pictures added to the shows I had only heard on the radio. Captain Midnight was one of my favorites. Through television I could see him. I was also coaxed by his sponsor, Ovaltine, into a morning breakfast drink.

Of course, that era was also the launching of Sputnik and a time of fear—what would be the results of the Cold War? Early in elementary school, we saw a film called *Duck and Cover* that told us how to protect ourselves in the event of a nuclear strike. I lived twenty miles from a major military establishment. *Frankenstein* seemed to capture all of the angst of technological advances.

I was amazed when later I learned that the full name of Shelley's book was *Frankenstein; or, The Modern Prometheus*. Indeed, her novel addressed classical themes and spoke to religious and medical themes of her own time, asking about the limits of our desires to create life. Knowing these simple facts about the author, her time, and how she sought to address her community profoundly

21

expanded my reading of the novel. In fact, its connection to the 1950s fascination with technology made even more sense.

As my quaint personal story shows, knowing about an author's time and purposes profoundly enriches understanding. The same is true with biblical studies. Biblical scholars have developed methods to assist us in understanding what was meant when a text was written. Their work is called *exegesis*, drawing on the Greek words meaning "to draw out of." Biblical exegesis is the effort to draw meaning out of a text. Biblical exegesis consists of a variety of methods including textual analysis, historical criticism, and theological analysis. The effort is to understand who wrote a text, when, in what context, to whom, and what was intended.

For example, the parable of the sower in Mark 4:1-20 begins, "A farmer went out to scatter seed. As he was scattering seed, some fell on the path; and the birds came and ate it" (4:3-4). As a child, the story was puzzling. Growing up in Indiana, I knew that farmers (and even gardeners) plowed fields, made furrows, and inserted seeds. Why would a "sower" throw seeds helter and skelter? We know the answer: that was the method of farming. Seeds were scattered on the ground. The miracle was watching plants grow among weeds and thorns. Knowing this makes the parable mean so much more.

For a more complicated example: Why are there two creation stories in Genesis? The first, in Genesis 1, describes a majestic creation of the whole world in seven days. Animals and humans are created on the sixth day. The whole story leads up to the day of rest connecting it to the Jewish practice of Sabbath. The second, beginning with Genesis 2:4b, tells the story of God's creation taking place in a garden. Here God creates a human and then from the human creates a partner—male and female. There are two stories with different emphases. In the same way, we know that throughout the Hebrew Bible some stories are repeated with differing emphases and differing commitments.

Knowing the process of authorship and the commitments of the editor assists us in understanding what is being said and why.

Why multiple takes on the same story? The answer the scholars tell us is that the text was edited over time as materials from differing oral traditions were added. Two traditions seeking to explain God's gift of creation are here merged side by side. Knowing the process of authorship and the commitments of the editor assists us in understanding what is being said and why.[1]

Another example: the letters to the Corinthians tell of Paul's efforts to build a thriving Christian community in major trading crossroads of the Roman Empire. Immediately we are connected with rival parties. The church consisted of people from a variety of social classes, probably some powerful Roman citizens, and some who had been slaves. Conflict resulted over hierarchy and practices of living and belief. Some seemed closer to traditional Roman practices and others to Jewish communal traditions. Paul speaks of rival parties dividing the community—"'I belong to Paul,' 'I belong to Apollos,' 'I belong to Cephas,' 'I belong to Christ'" (1 Cor 1:12). Knowing something of the history of the formation of the Christian community in Corinth, knowing the place of Corinth in the complex of Roman trade routes, and knowing what the conflict between these parties meant in the early church profoundly enhances the reading of the text.

Exegetical Approach to Teaching/ Leading Bible Study

Biblical scholars read multiple ancient languages and engage in the subtleties of literary and historical analysis. We ask, how can

23

we possibly participate in their work and do exegesis? Honestly, exegesis (interpretation) is simply a process of asking the right questions of a text. Resources for our work are available: Bible dictionaries, a study Bible, and a concordance.[2]

1. **Read the text carefully**—After beginning with prayer, read the text carefully. Note the themes and argument of the text. Note questions you have. Write them down. Note words about which you are confused. Note reactions or insights you have as you read the text.

2. **Turn to a study Bible or biblical dictionary**[3]—Read about the book and what scholars have concluded about its authorship, time of writing, and concerns it was addressing. Note the questions and concerns the scholars pose.

3. **Ask what kind of writing the text represents**— Throughout the Bible are many kinds of writing—songs, prayers, history, gospel, letters, laws, parables, and so on. The kind of writing profoundly affects the meaning. For example, the Gospels were written by believers to communicate the meaning of the life of Jesus. While some stories are repeated in different Gospels, they often have a different focus or meaning. Each Gospel writer had his own agenda. In contrast, songs and prayers are more metaphorical works. Is Song of Songs, for example, a conversation between two lovers or does it use the language of lovers to discuss one's relationship with God? Note the form of writing of the text.

4. **Ask what is known about authorship and context**— Read about the history behind the book; note the context and issues to which the author attends. For example, the Gospel of Matthew was probably written sometime in

the later first century between 75 and 85 CE. This would have been after the Roman/Jewish war when the temple in Jerusalem had been destroyed. The Jewish and Christian communities were separating over issues of belief and over questions of how to survive in a hostile Roman environment. It was probably written in Antioch of Syria, an extraordinarily diverse community filled with many ethnic groups where a rich conversation occurred among followers of Jesus and parties of Jewish believers.

5. **Ask what we know about the theological perspective and concern of the author**—Again looking at Matthew, we know the author of this book had an intimate understanding of the Jewish tradition. As he says throughout the Gospel, Jesus did not come to challenge the Law and the Prophets but to fulfill them (see Matt 5:17-20 and 22:40). "Don't even begin to think that I have come to do away with the Law and the Prophets. I haven't come to do away with them but to fulfill them" (Matt 5:17). Further commitments of the author are seen when we learn Jesus's life was told like a life of Moses—beginning with a risky birth (the killing of the innocents) and the proclaiming of the law (the Sermon on the Mount). The other Gospels either do not record these events or tell them in a different fashion.

6. **Now having insights on literary, historical, and theological commitments, reread the text**—In light of the information, how are the questions you had and the insights you had engaged? Read carefully. What might the author have meant in this particular text, what commitments was the author trying to communicate to readers? Share your insights and discuss the meanings you discover. You are thus biblical interpreters!

7. **Finally, ask what the text may be saying to your contemporary community**—The biblical writers were seeking to witness to their contemporaries and share the meaning of faith for the future. Matthew, for example, wanted his contemporaries to know Jesus. He knew this would make a difference for their futures. Another example: while Paul was seeking to communicate directly to a community conflict in Corinth, he knew these arguments would be discussed and shared later. Those who collected Paul's letters knew that the situations to which he spoke would arise elsewhere. In prayer and humility, ask what the text might mean for your life and your day and your community.[4] In fact, here we make a shift from asking questions of the texts to asking questions of ourselves—how do the texts interact with our lives?

Contributions of the Exegetical (Historical) Approach

Do you feel overwhelmed or do you think that this is possible? It may seem difficult, but I promise that the process gets clearer. For example, learning about Paul's writing or the purposes of the Gospels is cumulative. Our knowledge of the background and meanings of scripture grows. When we read Matthew again, we remember and draw on what we learned the last time we read it.

One advantage for churches that use the lectionary for worship and preaching is that certain passages are repeated every three years. Certain Old Testament passages, particular Gospels, and Letters are highlighted. The more we are exposed to texts and their backgrounds, the more we remember and connect.

The processes of historical biblical study and exegesis are rich, giving us background in the writing, commitments, and concerns of biblical authors. We would be greatly impoverished without this scholarship. Knowing about the cities of Corinth and Ephesus enriches our reading. Knowing the concerns and struggles of the Hebrew people as some returned to Jerusalem from the Babylonian exile enriches how we see the work of some of the final editors of the Torah. Or knowing the purposes of Matthew and Luke helps us understand their differences.

Yet, not all scholars agree. How can we base our faith on the seeming contradictions and changes in scholarship? Sometimes differing study Bibles and differing commentaries offer alternative views. How do we address that? Honestly, the only way is the way all scholars, pastors, and believers do. We read with prayer and humility. We seek to do the very best we can, asking what God is seeking to communicate with us in this time and in this place.

A tradition in Jewish scriptural interpretation helps. For generations, rabbis have been interpreting the texts of the Jewish scriptures for their contemporaries. The highest form of worship is sitting together seeking to understand what God would have us understand and be. Contemporary rabbinic scholars ask students to read a text, engage in exegesis, and also note how great rabbis interpreted it during several eras of time. The reader is then asked in humility to interpret the text informed by his or her own knowledge and the cumulative wisdom of the tradition.

In everyday living, this interpretive process is always the case. When looking into buying a new product, like a new refrigerator or a car, we read reviews, we visit stores, we talk to friends, we measure spaces, and then we make decisions. We assess differing information and opinions. In our faith life, the same is true, yet it is coupled with the wisdom of the long-standing history of interpretation, with the goodwill of our fellow believers, and with the graciousness of God. Historical exegetical study teaches all of God's children what questions to ask of a text.

Practice exegetical study, work with fellow believers, and grow in your understandings of the commitments of the first witnesses who prayerfully sought to tell us about the experiences of God in their lives.

Chapter Four

Book-by-Book Studies

Engaging the Purposes of a Book

The author of the Gospel of Matthew wanted to communicate to his community the powerful changes that had occurred in his life. The message that he had gained by following Jesus profoundly connected him with God and sent him on a mission. He defined his vocation, and that of all disciples, in the last chapter of the Gospel: "Go and make disciples of all nations . . . teaching them to obey everything that I've commanded you" (Matt 28:19-20). These words describe precisely what he was doing: seeking to make and teach disciples.

The Gospel of Matthew focuses on discipleship—disciples were those who gave food to the hungry, drink to the thirsty, welcome to a stranger, clothes to the naked, care to the sick, and visits to the imprisoned (Matt 25:31-46). Moreover, Jesus is described as the great teacher who gathers disciples, interpreting the law (Sermon on the Mount, Matt 5–7). "But everybody who hears these words of mine and doesn't put them into practice will be like a fool who built a house on sand. . . . When Jesus finished these words, the crowds were amazed at his teaching because he was teaching them like someone with authority" (Matt 7:26, 28-29). Knowing the purposes of the Gospel helps us to place it in context. Moreover, it helps us understand its message to us.

Another example: we know Paul's letters were written to particular situations in particular communities. Knowing the diversity and importance of Corinth in the Roman world, knowing the differing views the people confronted, and knowing the presence of other Christian witnesses teaching differing perspectives than Paul help us understand the content of this letter. We see real advice to real communities seeking faithfulness. Knowing the context of the writing of New Testament books helps us learn how important they were for the early church, how the issues facing the church then and now are important, and how we can seek to respond to these issues.

Book-by-book study is simply an extension of the historical and exegetical approach to biblical study. We all know that the Bible is itself a library. The Hebrew canon of the Jewish Tanakh included Torah, Prophets, and Writings. It ends with 2 Chronicles, the end of the Babylonian exile and the ongoing life of the Jewish community. The formulators of the Christian Bible shifted the ordering of the books. The order included Pentateuch (Torah), historical books, wisdom books, and prophets. The Christian canon of the Old Testament ends with the prophets, particularly Haggai, Zechariah, and Malachi with their foreshadowing of events to follow. Even this simple organization of the books of the Bible teaches much about the commitments of the Jewish and Christian communities—the continuation of a tradition or an expectation of renewal. Book-by-book study allows the reader to experience a sense of the whole and the particular place of each book in the whole.

Book-by-book study allows the reader to experience a sense of the whole and the particular place of each book in the whole.

For example, the great prophet Isaiah is a masterful, unified edited manuscript arising out of two very different times of persecution in the history of Israel. The book is very important as it is often quoted by Jesus and often appears in Jewish synagogue readings. Scholars know that Isaiah was a historical figure living in the eighth century BCE in Jerusalem during the Assyrian domination of that part of the world. Isaiah has direct access to the kings and leaders of the Hebrew people. His poetry, prose, history, and call for righteous living is clearly defined in the chapters 1–39 (what most scholars call First Isaiah). A second section, chapters 40–55 (Second Isaiah), refers to the later sixth century BCE Babylonian exile. The third section (Third Isaiah), 56–66, draws on multiple sources to define the hope that Israel will be restored and God will renew God's people.

Through a book study we see the work of an editor who wanted to define as clearly as possible the ongoing struggle for faithfulness and the interactions of God and God's people. This masterful compilation is not so much a history of Isaiah and Isaiah's time as a theological statement about the responsibility of the people for righteous living, God's continuing faithfulness, and the hope that God's future realm will become a reality.

Book-by-book study shows the place of this crucially important revelation of God with its theological commitments and meanings. We can then ask how it impacts our times and places.

Book-by-Book Approach to Teaching/Leading Bible Study

The steps of the book-by-book approach follow closely on those of the exegetical approach.

1. **Decision about a book to read or a set of books to read**—This decision is profound. It is an educational decision about what people want to explore. For example, we could decide to read the Pentateuch and join our Jewish brothers and sisters in exploring the key texts of the holy Torah. We could decide to read the letters of Paul to get a sense of the issues and commitments in various communities. We could compare our reading of Paul's letters with that of Acts, seeing then the theological commitments of Acts in telling the expanding story of the followers of Jesus. We could read the great prophets and explore their witness for "prophetic faith."[1] We could move through the Psalms to see the ways the Hebrew people communicated with, prayed to, and sang to God.

2. **Turn to a study Bible, commentary, or biblical dictionary**[2]—After prayer, read the introduction to the book in the study Bible, read the summary of the book in a Bible dictionary, and decide whether you will move through a commentary discussing the book section. These resources are very important for book-by-book study. They communicate the best wisdom of biblical scholars. Note the kinds of literature you expect to read (in Isaiah, for example, poetry, proclamation, story), the historical context of the author, and the author's theological commitments.

3. **Read the text carefully section by section as you proceed in your study**—The commentary is no substitute for immersing yourself in the text. As before, you should note questions, concerns, issues, and insights that come from the text.

4. **Ask together in the group how knowing the commitments of the writer and the book's context enhance your reading**—Explicitly note insights you have because of the research of the scholars—for example, the local and

pastoral concerns Paul was addressing. Also note places where you think scholars' introductions diverge from each other or they miss some insights that you saw in the text.

5. **Finally, ask what the text may be saying to your contemporary community**—We move from asking questions of the texts to asking questions of ourselves. Don't forget that while the reading of scripture is to understand the history of the people who saw themselves as children of God, the key reason for reading the scripture is to ask how it affects our call, vocation, and the life of our communities.

Contributions of the Book-by-Book Approach

I encourage you to enter into book-by-book study. I promise it will continue to strengthen your ability to do exegesis. It will give you a sense of the scope of the Bible and how sections of this library of holy books connect with and interact with each other. As before, the work of scholars and their disagreements both contribute to your insights and also can instill some anxiety about whether one understands the "truth" of the text. Yet, remember this anxiety may be fruitful as it keeps us questioning and searching for meanings.

Remember the Bible is the church's book. Church leaders saw its witness communicating relationships with God, the narratives enlivening their life and faith, and its word as a guide to living. We hope through the study of the Bible that we meet the living God and are able to grow in our faith, identity, and vocation as children following the ways of Jesus.

Chapter Five

Living the Themes of Faith

Studying Important Theological Concepts

A puzzling text is Jesus's interaction with Peter recorded in the Gospel of John. The resurrected Jesus has helped his disciples fish. Peter pulls the fish to shore. Jesus sets before them a meal of bread and fish.

Jesus then turns to Peter: "Simon son of John, do you love me more than these?" Peter answers, "Yes, Lord, you know I love you." Yet, once is not enough; Jesus asks him two more times, "Do you love me?" To which after the third inquiry, Peter answers, "Lord, you know everything; you know I love you" (John 21:15-17).

Why would Jesus ask Peter three times if he loved him? Didn't he believe him? Why would Jesus respond to Peter's proclamation with, "Feed my lambs," "Take care of my sheep," and "Feed my sheep" (John 21:15-17)? Of course, tradition has it that Peter denied Jesus three times, so is this a response to that? Moreover, the original Greek words used for "love" are different. What does the concept of love mean in the Christian witness?

For Jesus's Jewish colleagues and ancestors, the call of the Shema was to "love" God and neighbor. Is this the same meaning of love? To love God means devotion and trust in response to the grace and covenant that God extends to all of us—children of God. The love of neighbor means care, neighborliness, and justice—the common good. Is this meaning of love the same as Paul professed? "If . . . I don't have love, I'm a clanging gong or a clashing cymbal. . . . Love is patient, love is kind. . . . Love never fails" (1 Cor 13:1, 4, 8).

As we read the scriptures, we ask time and time again what a particular "concept" or "idea" means—what does it mean in the passage, how does that meaning connect with other passages, and to what does it call us today? For example, the call in much of scripture is for righteousness; many of the authors speak of repentance, and Paul says our ministry is reconciliation. God "has trusted us with this message of reconciliation. So we are ambassadors who represent Christ" (2 Cor 5:19-20). Are these the same? Or, some places we are told to "love" God and others to "fear" God. How do these relate? And Isaiah proclaims, "Don't be afraid, for I am your God" (Isa 41:10) and the angels tell the shepherds in the Gospel of Luke, "Don't be afraid! Look! I bring good news to you" (Luke 2:10). Are these the same meaning of fear?

A thematic approach to teaching and leading Bible study seeks to discover the meanings of key words and concepts.

A thematic approach to teaching and leading Bible study seeks to discover the meanings of key words and concepts. Exegesis assists us. As we know, words carry different meanings over time and in different contexts. Thematic study enriches and expands our understanding of the theology—read "big ideas"—that is important to thoughtful readers of the biblical texts.

Thematic Approach to Teaching/ Leading Bible Study

The steps of the thematic approach include the following:

1. **Read the text carefully**—The question of a meaning of a word or concept comes from a particular text we are reading or studying. We are usually also aware that it is used elsewhere. Prayerfully read the text and state what you think it means in this passage—using all the exegetical questions of author and context.

2. **Make a decision about a theme or concept to explore**— This decision is profound. What is the word or concept we need to explore? Note why the issue is important. Think about what questions, concerns, and hopes motivate you. Answers to the question of why they motivate you will help you connect your learnings to your living.

3. **Turn to a biblical dictionary, concordance, or study Bible**[1]—Does this advice sound like a broken record? These resources are so helpful. We do not study alone; we have a long tradition of colleagues and friends in the faith who have sought to understand the meanings of texts and offer insights. Study is a communal process. First, turn to a biblical dictionary to see if a word is defined. Often the dictionary itself will tell you the differing meanings and from where they are drawn. Second, turn to a concordance (either a separate book or online concordance or to a concordance section in a study Bible). For example, in the *The CEB Study Bible* there are references for *love*, *loved*, and *loving* (609–10). A concordance points you to passages where a word is explicitly used. *The CEB Study Bible* notes nine passages where "love of neighbor" is explicitly used (610). As you study, simply decide a few passages you will explore.

4. **Read carefully some of the alternative texts suggested by the concordance**—If you are working in a group, you can share the tasks of looking up passages and making decisions about what they mean. Read some of the passages aloud and list the meanings.

5. **Share the meanings that you have found**—Indeed, share and cluster the meanings, noting contrasting ideas. For example, "loving neighbor": in *The CEB Study Bible*, the texts begin with a reference to the book of Leviticus, where the text defines that a faithful believer is to "love your neighbor" (Lev 19:18). This particular reference seems to be quoted by Jesus in the Sermon on the Mount (Matt 5:43), in his conversation with first the rich man (Matt 19:19), and later with a group of Pharisees (Matt 22:34-40; a same or similar incident is reflected in Mark 12:28-33 and Luke 10:25-37). Clearly Jesus here embodies a Jewish tradition. It is also shared by Paul in Galatians 5:14 and Romans 13:9. Finally, "loving neighbor" is defined as the most important task of "scripture" in the letter of James (2:8).

   Without a doubt, this quick survey of very diverse literature demonstrates the importance of the Shema for the Jewish community, for Jesus's preaching and ministry, and for the early church. In fact, a distinguishing mark of the early Christian community was its faithfulness to loving neighbor and risking participating in the ministries of care, healing, freedom, forgiveness, and new life.[2]

6. **Finally, ask what the text may be saying to your contemporary community**—Ask together what you have learned about the meaning of this word or concept and what its import may be for your own living. If loving God and neighbor is the heart of the Torah tradition, re-expressed and honored by Jesus, and lived in the early

Christian community, then isn't it the call of the ministry of discipleship?

This conversation points again to the markers of the realm of God that Jesus saw. These are also markers of faithfulness today. Remember, they are the following:

- healing the sick,

- giving sight to the blind,

- offering hearing to those who are deaf,

- forgiving those who have sinned,

- proclaiming release to prisoners,

- preaching the good news to the poor, the least of these,

- restoring community, and

- enacting shalom.[3]

Contributions of the Big Ideas/ Theological Concepts Approach

A thematic study enlarges our understandings of the key concepts of the Bible and how they can become key concepts for faith and living. Above we saw through a very quick study the consistency of certain meanings; other places we will see the diversity of meanings. These offer us options to consider and questions to seek to answer.

I appreciate greatly when our church publishing houses offer studies that point us to some of the richest and most meaningful terms of the faith. DISCIPLE Bible studies offer both a sweeping survey of the Bible and an explicit focus on the meaning of discipleship today (cokesbury.com/disciple). It has profoundly enriched the understanding of the term *disciple* for over a million students.

The new Covenant Bible Study has taken the concept of God's covenant with God's people as the heart of their new in-depth Bible study (covenantbiblestudy.com). Through in-depth Bible study, the series connects us with a significant portion of the whole Bible, while at the same time enriching our understanding of concepts like "creating, living, and trusting" the covenant with God and others. It moves from understanding God's creation of the world and God's covenant with humans to how we are to honor this enduring relationship in our everyday lives.

Thematic Bible study continues to enhance and enrich our understandings of the "big ideas" and richest concepts at the heart of our faith. We see honestly some of the differences of interpretations in the biblical text itself and can better understand some of the disagreements in the faith community today. We see how a priestly call to honor, live, and embody the tradition may conflict with a prophetic call focusing on the pain to which certain groups of people are subjected, and wisdom faith efforts to find a new way in a new time that may stretch the spirit of the tradition.

Chapter Six

Lectionary Studies

Connecting Study, Worship, and Service

The Revised Common Lectionary is a pattern of scripture readings for Sunday worship used in many mainline Protestant denominations as well as the Roman Catholic Church. While there are some differences of emphasis, many of the lections—an Old Testament reading, a psalm, an epistle, and a Gospel reading—are the same. The lectionary follows a three-year cycle where the Synoptic Gospels (Matthew, Mark, and Luke) anchor the readings, with many selections from the Gospel of John appearing, often in high holy days. The lections/readings are connected to the liturgical year beginning in Advent and continuing through Christmas, Epiphany, Lent, Easter, and ordinary time.[1]

The lectionary provides a regular pattern for the study of scripture. Even more, it integrates texts with personal and congregational experience. Preaching, worship, the liturgical year, and the flow of congregational life are connected. A study group can read the texts in preparation for worship, read them with the preacher of the week and assist with the content generated for the sermon, or read them after preaching as a means of going deeper and reflecting on additional meanings for the community of faith.

In fact, in one congregation I know, a group of people meet during the week before the sermon on Sunday. They individually study the lections/readings at home. Through their conversation, key themes connecting their lives to the biblical passages are identified. They share the themes in preparation for worship. The whole worship experience is thus shaped by an intimate connection of people and texts from the Bible. Furthermore, this congregation allows the studied and proclaimed scripture passages to influence its mission by asking what call to ministry and discipleship has been heard in the studying and preaching. From speaking with those who are regular attenders in lectionary groups, they witness that study prepares them for worship, connects their daily lives with the meanings of scripture, and provides a regular discipline of asking what the text means for themselves and their communities.

The Revised Common Lectionary is the most used lectionary. There are curricula developed for use with it. See, for example, Cokesbury's Advent and Lenten studies, *Spark*, the *Whole People of God*, and *Feasting on the Word*.[2] Each provides study helps for the chosen lections and resources for worship and devotion. Most major denominations provide lectionary resources for study, for worship, for devotion, and for sermon preparation.[3]

The primary contribution of the lectionary study is the integration of study, worship, liturgical year, congregational practices, and personal living.

In addition to *The Revised Common Lectionary*, there are also others, used by fewer congregations, that fulfill particular educational purposes. An example is the *Narrative Lectionary* developed by faculty at Luther Seminary in Minnesota.[4] It offers a four-year narrative cycle moving sequentially through the history of Israel, the four Gospels, Acts, and the Pauline Letters.

Lectionary Approach to Teaching

The lectionary approach is basically an exegetical approach to scripture focused on the meaning of the texts for the life and ministry of a congregation and its members. Note the connection here of the lives of believers, the life of a congregation, the events of the wider world, and the biblical witness.

Lectionary study groups find themselves growing in knowledge and care for their members and for the ministry of the congregation. They usually work best when a member takes responsibility for planning the study and when each member reads the texts and prepares at home.

1. **Begin with prayer**—Since the purpose of study is to make the connection between living and God's witness heard through the scripture, groups begin with prayer.

2. **Sharing of events in the lives of the members and of the congregation**—Take time to share important events in members' lives and in the congregation. Knowing these provides an opportunity to grow in support and care, but even more, it begins the process of assisting people to connect life, study, and faith.

3. **Read the texts for study**—While these have probably already been read at home, reading them again focuses attention. After both prayer and personal sharing, new questions and insights jump out for the members.

4. **Explore each text**—A designated group member leads in exploring each text. Comments and questions as well as background (history, authorship, theology) will be shared in conversation. Make sure to note questions and concerns and insights that members have.

5. **Seeing connections in the text**—Lectionary texts have been chosen with a purpose—the liturgical year of the congregation. Some passages of scripture are used fully; others are edited for congregational reading. Name connections among the texts. You will probably find the connections that caused the designers of the lectionaries to bind the texts together, but in light of your sharing, the life of the congregation, and events in the surrounding world, new insights may be named.

6. **Ask what the text may be saying to you and your community**—Through the exegetical study, the sharing of lives, the discussion in the group, the emphases of the liturgical year, and the realities and decisions facing the congregation, note how these lead to insights for living. As the study draws to a close, provide an opportunity for people to name commitments that they are making. One role of an ongoing study group often is accountability. A group of colleagues and friends can continue to ask each other, how is it with your soul? How is your faith life growing? What struggles are you encountering?

7. **Close with prayer.**

Contributions of the Lectionary Approach

The primary contribution of the lectionary study is the integration of study, worship, liturgical year, congregational practices, and personal living. Note that as we have moved forward through our study of the last few models, increasingly the focus has been living a life informed by biblical wisdom. While such integration of life and text can happen in any approach, integrative approaches like the lectionary focus on it. As noted in the introduction to this book, committed groups help us practice connecting questions of life and biblical texts to the natural processes of faith reflection.[5]

The biggest issue that lectionary groups find is the interconnection of texts themselves. As stated, the focus of the most widely used lectionary is the liturgical year. Bible passages don't always cohere easily. Members of groups sometimes in frustration ask what makes these connect. Haven't we heard pastors comment, "The texts I received for today are very difficult, the connections are stretched; I'll try to make them whole (or, I'll simply focus on one)"?[6]

Nevertheless, the lectionary provides a formula for reading through much of the Bible. It is therefore comprehensive. It also attends to connections among biblical texts, everyday living, worship, and service.

Chapter Seven

Praying the Scriptures

Personal, Group, and Family Devotions

The psalmist prays,

Lord, you have examined me.
>   You know me.
You know when I sit down and when I stand up.
>   Even from far away, you comprehend my plans.
You study my traveling and resting.
>   You are thoroughly familiar with all my ways.
. . . .
Examine me, God! Look at my heart!
>   Put me to the test! Know my anxious thoughts!
Look to see if there is any idolatrous way in me,
>   then lead me on the eternal path! (Psalm 139:1-3, 23-24)

The scriptures are filled with some of the richest prayers—personal lamentations focusing on loss, corporate petitions asking God for help, personal cries for God's partnership in the burdens of life, and joyous prayers of thanksgiving.

For generations, people of faith have called on God to examine and guide them. The scriptures emerged in communities seeking to understand God's presence. Through these writings, persons of faith witnessed to the impact God had on their living.

This dynamic process of longing and witnessing has continued from the past to our present. In fact, we Christians speak about the guidance of the Holy Spirit—a "comforter" to teach us and help us know God's love, care, and call (John 14:26).

The scriptures are a place we turn to help guide us to understand God's love and dream today. Yet, we all know that the shift from the meanings of the past to the realities of the present is often difficult. You may have experienced it during work with the previous methods of biblical study. Each ended with this statement: *Ask what the text or passage may be saying to your contemporary community or to you.*

Yet, while some biblical writings speak powerfully and directly to us, others puzzle us. By itself, exegetical study does not always help us bridge past and future. It tells us much about the context of the writing and the purposes of authors. Yet, we search for more than this. We ask, What is God's redemptive experience for today, on what hopes can we depend, and to what future will we commit? With the psalmist we hunger: "Teach me your way, LORD, / so that I can walk in your truth. / Make my heart focused / only on honoring your name" (Ps 86:11; see also Ps 25).

To entertain discovery by seeking the voice of God is the hope of praying the scriptures.

One historic way persons have sought to answer these questions is by praying the scriptures. A primary pattern has been *lectio divina* (simply translated, "divine reading"), which arose in the abbeys of St. Benedict. The process of *lectio divina* was to pray the scripture over and over, simultaneously listening with the heart and the head. Its elements usually consisted of the following:

- reading or hearing a text,

- identifying where the text speaks to you or how it makes you feel,

- considering the meanings or questions raised,

- praying for wisdom,

- rereading or relistening to the text, and

- again considering meanings, praying, and continuing the process until one feels or knows a conviction.

My first experience with *lectio divina* was in a Cistercian abbey, Abbey of Gethsemani in Bardstown, Kentucky. A retreat weekend was filled with texts to read, scheduled times of prayer, listening to the scriptures even during meals, and meeting with a spiritual guide. As Father Thomas Merton, a noted Trappist monk, commented, retreats like ones at Gethsemani provide a place apart "to entertain silence in the heart and listen for the voice of God—to pray for your own discovery."[1] To entertain discovery by seeking the voice of God is the hope of praying the scriptures.

Yet, there is a balance; we all know we can be misled. We do tell lies to ourselves. We make ourselves believe we are justified for doing things when we are not. How do we deal with the balance?

- One element is to pray texts in the midst of communities. Our communities of accountability support and challenge. My own experience is the penetrating questions of my spiritual guides and covenant group members have helped me keep focused.

- A second element is the rich tradition of biblical scholarship. Texts often question us and won't let us get away with easy answers.

47

- A third element is entering the process in prayer and humility. Knowing God will call us into question.[2]

A Jesuit scholar, William Thompson, offers a three-step process of praying the scriptures: (1) getting to know the passage through study and scholarship, (2) praying the passage, and (3) further study.[3] Combining Thompson's rich scholarship and the historic practice of *lectio divina*, let me suggest an approach.[4]

Praying the Scripture Approach to Teaching Bible Study

The steps of a prayer approach include the following:

1. **Read a text carefully**—As described before, read the text, list words, comments, questions, and insights that arise.

2. **Pray the text**—In a spirit of prayer, read or listen to the text again. Listen to your heart. Note a word or phrase that arises or calls for reflection.

3. **Meditate on a chosen word or phrase**—Consider why that phrase or word is important or calling to you. Note whatever has happened or is happening in your life to which that phrase could be connecting. Share you insights with a colleague or friend.

4. **Pray the text again**—Again, pray the text, listen to it, and note what comes to awareness, to insight.

5. **Study the text**—If alone, in personal devotion, take some time to engage the historical and thematic study of the text (exegesis). If working in an ongoing study group, ask someone to prepare a brief historical background of

the passage and share with the group. Take some time to study the meanings and context of the text.

6. **Pray the text again**—Seek to enter into the text, to see its events, hear its meanings, smell its aromas, and encounter its expectations. Ask as you pray, "Teach me your way, LORD, / so that I can walk in your truth. / Make my heart focused / only on honoring your name" (Ps 86:11).

7. **Meditate on and share the questions, insights, and meanings of the prayer**—If alone, write brief ideas or comments to yourself that you will share with another (like a spiritual guide or director). If in the group, share insights, convictions, hopes, or commitments arising from the prayer and study process first with a partner and then in the group.

8. **If in a group, note group commitments or insights that emerge**—As the group moves to the end of their time together, after their sharing, ask if there are patterns, commitments, hopes, convictions, or insights that have emerged.

9. **Close with prayer**—I recommend again the use of the prayer of Psalm 86: "Teach me your way, LORD, / so that I can walk in your truth. / Make my heart focused / only on honoring your name" (Ps 86:11).

Contributions of a Praying the Scriptures Approach

The practice of praying the scripture acknowledges that scripture is a witness to the word of God calling us to faithfulness—to dynamically embody hopes and aspirations of it in a new day and a new time. The practice also recognizes the richness and power of historical exegetical study. The connecting of prayer and study engages our minds, hearts, and bodies in seeking faithfulness and insight. We honor the tradition, we respect the witnesses whose voices ring through scripture, and without a doubt we recognize and acknowledge that biblical study for faith is an act of prayer and humility. May God examine us and look at our hearts. May God put us to the test and point us in the ways of faithfulness.

Chapter Eight

Story and Scripture

*Drawing on African American
Cultural Resources*

Living biblical faith means that a person's daily life is connected to the call of God. *Faith* is an active word. Faith names our trust in God, our knowledge that God continues to seek us, and our commitments to work to embody God's hopes for us and our world. Yet, connecting daily living and the biblical story is difficult. Each of us is a complicated mix of identities and commitments.

For example, I am a father, a husband, a grandfather, a child of working-class parents, a product of Indiana public schools, a US citizen, an ordained United Methodist pastor, a seminary professor, and a resident of a multicultural suburb near Chicago. I am ethnically of a mixed heritage—English, German, Scotch-Irish, Dutch, and so on—yet in the United States, I am "white." I belong to a set of professional and voluntary associations that take my time and energy (for example, editing the journal *Religious Education*). Moreover, I have friends and acquaintances from other cultures and religious groups who rightfully expect certain things of me, including knowledge of their traditions, respect, and collegiality.

Our identities are complex, for we are part of peoples and groups. A friend from a small country in Africa tells me about the major tribal groups in his culture. How one is treated is clearly affected by one's roles and accomplishments, yet one is always known by one's tribal heritage. No matter where we live, our contexts and histories profoundly define us and our questions. In the next three chapters, we will draw on cultural resources from around the world to help us explore approaches to biblical study that connect the Bible and life.

The first is drawn from the African American tradition in the United States. Having participated in the major and hope-filled social changes in the 1960s, Dr. Anne Streaty Wimberly of Interdenominational Theological Center saw the continuing realities of racism and of a lack of economic opportunity. She knew the long destructive reach of the consequences of slavery—of being dehumanized and brought by force and violence to this country. Therefore, she looked for patterns of hope and resilience that empowered people to work for transformation.

People connect faith, the biblical story, their cultures, and their lives through narrative (story).

She found these by examining historical slave narratives—memoirs of those who were enslaved—and contemporary congregational practices. Story-linking was the approach she discovered and described.[1] People, she argued, connect faith, the biblical story, their cultures, and their lives through narrative. Biblical study and Christian education can empower people to work to transform the world when the goals of Christian education are "liberation and vocation." Christian education is therefore motivated by the following commitments:

1. knowing one's life as gift—being a valued human being,

2. ability to maintain basic necessities of life,

3. being equal partners and beneficiaries in life-building processes of a nation,

4. being treated justly and respectfully,

5. seeing possibilities and breaking out of restricted ways of thinking and acting,

6. sharing stories with self and others,

7. being changed by God in Jesus Christ, and

8. being aware of other's needs and willing to respond.[2]

In other words, empowering biblical education focuses on how people are valued as human beings, transformed by God, and become partners in building a community and nation that cares for all.

African American Story-Linking Approach to Teaching

Story-linking connects histories, communities, and experiences of the African American heritage with the biblical story. The process begins either with an experience drawn from a person's life or the community or a story from the biblical witness. Throughout the approach the following questions are asked:

- "What are you doing with your life as a Christian?

- What is God calling you to be and do?

- What meaning and purpose do you assign to your life as a Christian?"[3]

The elements of the story-linking method include the following:[4]

1. **Begin with prayer**—The purpose of study is to live the vocation God is freeing us to live and do.

2. **Engage the everyday story**—Begin with life stories, with concrete life events. Attend to their social context, relationships, and meanings. Note: What questions or challenges are raised?

3. **Engage the Christian faith story in the Bible**—Here there is a choice: explore either a biblical story scheduled for the day or name a particular story that seems to parallel the everyday story being considered. Explore the text fully. Remember some persons in the group have differing knowledge about and experience with the Bible. As the Bible is read, think about both what God did in the past and what God is doing today.

4. **Engage the Christian faith stories in the African American heritage**—Explore the faith heritage and stories of members of the group about how their ancestors, either personally or publicly, engaged these events before. Remember to focus on the elements of a liberating faith, knowing that God works with God's people to free them to be children of God. Think about the liberation and vocation forebears lived.

5. **Engage in Christian ethical decision making**—The goal of the process is to explore options for deciding and acting in your present. Reflect critically on and decide what you are being called to do and be as Christians—on vocation. Share together a hope or a commitment you seek to live as a result of the study. Make commitments. Hold each other responsible.

Contributions of the Story-Linking Approach

This approach seeks to name a natural, developed approach to study and living that is present in many African American churches. It stresses the dimensions of liberation at the heart of the biblical witness and of the African American story of struggle in the United States.

Moreover, it acknowledges and proclaims that we all are connected to cultural stories and patterns. We have witnesses who have preceded us, providing models of faithfulness. These witnesses guide us; they show us options. The power of the approach is how it connects living, culture, and the biblical witness. It directs the gaze of the learners to God's ongoing actions for liberation and empowerment.

Over the years as this approach has been shared in the classes I have taught, all students, even those who are not of African American heritage, have been able to recognize that they, too, are embedded in cultural stories. Patterns deeply resident in our cultural stories define reality. While many cultures do not have such an explicit experience with oppression and may in fact be connected to perpetrators of oppression, every person learns that we need to attend explicitly to the realities of our cultures.

While it is totally inappropriate for other cultures to assume the heritage offered by Dr. Wimberly in her approach for African Americans, students have, and I promise you will, become aware of stories, heroes, perspectives, and directions that both define and empower them. We are asked, What are the primary themes God has injected into our cultures? What do we claim, for what do we need to ask forgiveness, and what do we accept? Our heritages clearly affect our identities and our vocations as person of faith in our time and place. They focus our attention. For example, a student from Korea talked about the experience of oppression and rape his people experienced in World War II. He mentioned the heroes of his Christian community who sacrificed their lives for justice. He draws on these resources is his study and his ministry.

Our cultures shape our identities. How do they affect what we see and what we deny? How do they provide options for our teaching and learning and our faithfulness? If we are truthful, the faith becomes more deeply rooted in the persons that we are. We seek God's call to be God's children and live in community with others.

We all, no matter majority or minority, need to struggle with our cultures and their impacts on how we know, behave, and think about God.

An important footnote: sometimes people in the majority culture deny that they have a unique culture. They simply think that others have culture and that they are the norm. For example, in the United States, white and European-heritage people are presently the norm. (I may be ethnically mixed, yet I am still white and male and have been given advantages.) Whiteness is a culture. We all, no matter majority or minority, need to struggle with our cultures and their impacts on how we know, behave, and think about God. This approach calls us to take seriously the power of culture.

God is working in our lives to free us from anything that keeps us from being faithful and mutual children of God. To what is God calling us and what decisions do we make? That is the challenge of story-linking.

My students witness that the approach has value across cultures if we listen carefully, seek honesty, and honor the gifts, problems, and pain we discover. We cannot really answer the questions of vocation, decision making, or faithfulness unless we acknowledge and engage cultures and their patterns of meaning and learning. Only then can we ask, What are we doing with our lives as Christians?

Chapter Nine

Theology for Daily Living

Drawing on Latin American Cultural Resources

"Theology at sunset" is a provocative metaphor developed by the ministries of small congregations in Latin America to describe the process of learning to live faithfully in everyday experience. It further connects our reflections about Bible study and culture to the realities of the global church.

Each day, people living in barrios would leave to travel to work in the central cities. As they returned home at night they would often gather for sustenance and faith sharing with families and friends in small congregations (*comunidad eclesial de base*, or base communities) of approximately twenty persons each.[1] Together they would celebrate their lives, even if they were hard and difficult.

As these workers and their families would gather, they would reflect on the events of the day in light of the biblical witness, or, in their words, practice "theology at sunset." "They relate the experiences of their day (wages insufficient to provide food, shelter, and clothing; no medical care; inadequate education; political brutality) to the Scriptures. Their reflection calls forth a response—an action expressed politically, or through seeking a change in the oppressive structure of the status quo."[2] Thus, study, sharing, and reflection are connected with worship, sacraments, and ministry.

When the people gather in the base communities, scripture is read. The people comment on it in light of their experiences as children of God. The leader, the *animator*, has studied the text and its meanings. Through invitation, listening, and conversation, the leader *animates* the people to connect the integrity of the scripture with the integrity of their lives. In fact, convinced that God speaks through the scriptures, the people search for God's call to them in their day.

A profound example of the method of the base communities was published by Ernesto Cardenal in *The Gospel in Solentiname*.[3] Solentiname is a group of islands in Lake Nicaragua. Sermons were dialogic—engaged conversations among people and leader about the meanings of scripture and the call of God to wholeness, justice, and community. Here we see a talented animator, Fr. Cardenal, who has studied the text and knows the people, asking questions to connect living and faith. Fr. Cardenal knew that their lives were connected to a particular place and history—a particular archipelago, in a country divided, in a poor region of the world, and controlled by the economic realities of the Americas.

Broad generalizations about faith would not address the people's realities. For example, as they talked about Jesus's interaction with the rich young man (the one who had fulfilled all explicit prescriptions in the Shema but was unable to love God and neighbor more than his possessions, Matt 19:16-22), their conversation ranged widely, speaking of their poverty, noting the haughtiness of many for whom they worked, and eventually focused on the hope of the realm of God. God called them to steward what they had and work together for new life in their own community. The gospel helped them recognize that they too were honored children of God and agents of hope.[4]

Biblical research shows that these meetings of base communities were very similar to what occurred in many early Christian communities.[5] For example, the early Roman church was extraordinarily diverse, including Gentiles and Jews as well as persons of several social strata. These "churches" were really small house churches where persons knew each other and intimately shared living and believing. Many of the Christians had low-level jobs dyeing fabrics in the Roman textile industry. Many lived in tenement sections of Rome in wooden and mud apartment buildings, often poorly constructed. On the first floor were businesses, perhaps even the business in which they worked. As the floors extended up, the poorest with large families were accommodated on top floors, in small rooms, without the heat or water of the homes of wealthier citizens. Often Christians who shared the buildings would work during the day and gather together at nights, sharing in a common meal consisting of worship, thanksgiving, prayer, listening to the scriptures (the law and gospel) and telling the stories of Jesus. Their conversations focused on living as faithful followers of Christ.

Paul's letter to the Romans, written as he approached Rome for trial, seeks to communicate to this diverse community his understandings of Christian living. Evidence shows that while these early Christians in many ways lived as their Roman neighbors, yet in other ways, they were very different because they cared for each other, offered healing to those who were sick, paid the price of freedom for indentured slaves, and lived in communities connected to the redemptive new life offered in the ministry of Jesus.[6]

While this approach to connecting the Bible to daily life is empowering, we need to remember that it is shaped, even in the early Roman example, by the economic realities of exploitation. The questions those in the base communities, in Solentiname, in Rome, and even in Galilee in Jesus's day asked were about how they could live in a world where the powerful controlled wealth. Is there hope amidst increased taxation, low wages, inadequate health care, and limited life chances? This reality focused the questions that the believers asked of their lives.

Through this approach, we are clear that Bible study is characterized by questions we ask of both the texts we are studying and of the lives we bring to the study. What is troubling, focusing, or defining our lives profoundly affects what we see. For example, I taught a class where we looked at Psalm 137—the psalm of petition sung by the Hebrew people when they were prisoners in Babylon. The passage reads,

> Alongside Babylon's streams,
>   there we sat down,
>   crying because we remembered Zion.
> We hung our lyres up
>   in the trees there
>   because that's where our captors asked us to sing;
>   our tormentors requested songs of joy:
>   "Sing us a song about Zion!" they said.
> But how could we possibly sing
>   the LORD's song on foreign soil? (Ps 137:1-4)

A member of the class, a young woman who was a recent refuge from Liberia, broke into tears because the psalm described her experience. Captured in the revolution at home, she had been taunted to sing the songs of her captors. This deeply faithful woman, who had joined forces with other women protesting the conflict, connected her living to the Hebrews in Babylon. In fact, she rejected the actions suggested at the end of the psalm, where the captives in Babylon pray for retribution: "Daughter Babylon, you destroyer, / a blessing on the one who pays you back / the very deed you did to us!" (Ps 137:8). She told us that she understood the anger, that she had it, yet she witnessed that retribution did not help. In fact, retribution pushed her people deeper and deeper into violence.

The task for this approach is intimately connecting everyday faith and social experience with the scripture and finding a particular call to ministry in a particular time.

Some of us may share the social situation of those in the base communities or the early Roman tenement churches; many others of us do not. The task for this approach is intimately connecting everyday faith and social experience with the scripture and finding a particular call to ministry in a particular time. We need to be clear about what questions we ask of a text. Moreover, our forebears and colleagues from the base communities and the Roman church would tell us not to neglect the elements of exploitation, power, and class as we put questions to the text. How do they name your reality or action?

Theology for Daily Living Approach to Bible Study

The elements of this approach to teaching include the following:

1. **Begin at home with study of the texts**—Explore the texts using all the biblical resources at hand. Ask one person in particular to be prepared as a leader having engaged in study of the meaning of the text in its time. Ask questions of social status, exploitation, power, and political control of the text. What social situation is shaping the text? (I suggest you take turns and share this task around the group.)

2. **When you gather, begin with prayer, for we are seeking to live what God expects us to be and do**—We are seeking to name and clarify the questions we are asking from our lives and to our lives.

3. **Share the events of the week with each other—note that you are doing theology, that you are reading the text in light of the questions your lives ask**—Let one of the group or several in the group point to questions their everyday living have brought to them. Again, do not neglect economic and political realities.

4. **Read the biblical text for the day**—As you read it, listen to its call in your life. Think in particular how the personal and social realities facing you sound in light of the text.

5. **Have the leader for the day share findings of the study**—Have the leader share the social situation of the text.

6. **Engage in conversation**—Probe your lives and the text. Let the personal and social realities of your lives and the personal and social realities of the text connect with each other. You may want to focus on one question asked by one person that seems important in the group.

7. **Finally, ask to what God is calling you in light of your study and sharing**—Talk about this question in the group. Also ask each member to write some ideas for himself or herself. Ask if there are any commitments the group is willing to make. Ask each member, as he or she is willing, to share a commitment they are making as a result of your study.

8. **Thank God in prayer for being with you in your studying, reflecting, and committing.**

Contributions of the Base Communities Approach to Scripture

Like the story-linking model, this "theology at sunset" approach calls us to question the text and our lives from the perspectives of the cultural and social realities that surround us. It connects us to the wider realities of the global church and the diverse circumstances in which Christians live and have faith. The approach asks us to be clear about the questions, perspectives, and life stance we are bringing to the text.

The experiences of our lives profoundly shape what we see and where we focus. If an experience of loss is present, loss shapes what we focus on in our lives and in the texts. In turn, an experience of betrayal focuses the questions brought to the study, as does an experience of joy, of new birth, of trauma, of exploitation, or of hope. More so than the other approaches we have studied to this point, this approach asks us the most significant personal questions and attends to the social contexts and economic realities of our lives and communities.[7]

"Theology at sunset" or theology in daily living is a powerful method that integrates the personal and the public, the interpersonal and the social, into faithfully interpreting scripture and faithfully living our lives as children of God.

Chapter Ten

See-Judge-Act

Study for Mission and Vocation

What is my vocation, my calling, as a Christian person? How am I to live faith in the everyday? What is the mission of the church in the community? These are crucial questions for a faithful person and for our congregations.

Often, however, we move through life almost in automatic mode—simply repeating the ordinary. The same is true of many congregations. Without intentional effort to ask these questions of mission and to work toward answers, the ordinary reigns. The advantage of ongoing Bible studies is that we have opportunity to ask these questions over and over as we focus our attention on vocation and mission.

That is the intention of the see-judge-act approach. Originally developed in the early twentieth century by a Belgian priest, Fr. Joseph Cardijn, in his efforts for worker justice, see-judge-act later appeared in the mid-1960s in the grand encyclical of Pope John the XXIII on social issues and human dignity, *Mater et Magistra.*[1] This encyclical called the church to work with civil governments to provide sufficient support for the thriving of citizens and the world:

> There are three stages which should normally be followed in the reduction of social principles into practice. First, one reviews the concrete situation; secondly, one forms a judgment

on it in the light of these same principles; thirdly, one decides what in the circumstances can and should be done to implement these principles. These are the three stages that are usually expressed in the three terms: look, judge, act.[2]

Since its wide circulation, this method has become a primary approach for denominational communities, both Protestant and Catholic, to discern mission. For example, The National Plan for Hispanic/Latino Ministry of the United Methodist Church defines see-judge-act in the following manner:

> In order to be in effective ministry one must be willing to see the social reality in which Hispanics/Latinos live. Seeing, however, is never enough. One must take the next step of critically evaluating the social reality before us. As people of Christian faith, this critical evaluation must always be done through the lens of Holy Scripture and faith. Finally, one must determine what action one will take. Action is always grounded in an understanding of God's will for God's people. The ultimate goal is the transformation of persons and the world in the name and power of Christ Jesus.[3]

Critical reflection, social analysis, and theological reflection unite to discern to what vocation and mission God is calling us.

Seeing means looking deeply at the realities that surround us—then judging what is happening and acknowledging publicly what we will commit ourselves to do.

See-judge-act can help us attend to the various aspects of our lives—families and friends, schools and places of employment, congregations, and communities. Seeing means looking deeply at the realities that surround us (the more concrete this happens the better). We then judge what is happening using all of our resources—our knowledge, reason, and study. Finally, we acknowledge publicly, so we can be held accountable, to what we will commit ourselves and do.

We all seek to live our faiths in a world that is often conflicted. Values and convictions compete for our attention. Among multiple competing realities, we seek pathways to faithfulness. We pray for discernment. We study the Bible and our lives together to find ways as persons of faith and as congregations to commit ourselves *purposefully* to the way of Jesus in the world.[4]

See-Judge-Act Approach to Bible Study

The elements of the see-judge-act approach can begin with a study of a passage of scripture or with reflection on a life experience. Yet, both scripture and experience are to be engaged.[5]

1. **Begin with prayer**—Honestly ask God to assist us in seeing, judging, and doing as we read and study. (By the way, you can do this at home individually before you come together as a group. That will enrich and enhance group reflections.)

2. **See**—Ask of the text what is happening, why it is happening, and who is being affected. In prayer, ask, what does this text point me to see and hear in my life and my community? Be willing to risk. Name a concern or a commitment in your life or community. Then ask the questions again of your life experience: "What is happening, why is it happening, and who is being affected?"

3. **Judge**—As you gather the insights acquired by "seeing" the scripture and your life experience, ask, why am I seeing this, what connects them? Share what you think about all of this. "Name what your values, your beliefs, and your faith say about this. Consider together what do you think should be happening."

4. **Act/Discern**—Be willing to risk again. Too often we circle around and around avoiding decision. Name something in your life and community to which this discussion has called you. Note what you "would like to change in the long term, . . . what action you will take in the short term." Finally, be strategic: ask who can help you and what steps you will take.

5. **Close with commitments and prayer**—Out loud again name the action(s). Reassure each other that you will follow up and look at how new see-judge-act moments question, enhance, or focus discernment. See-judge-act is an ongoing reflective activity.

Again, this method can begin with an issue or with scripture. Any personal issue you are facing or any decision facing the congregation can be examined through see-judge-act. Some personal and some congregational decisions require time and a lot of reflection. For example, this process is excellent for a major congregational decision. Simply (and it may not be as simple as it sounds) make sure that at every point, scripture and experience are being connected.

Contributions of
See-Judge-Act Approach

Discernment of faithfulness is the task of this approach. As we engage in acts of discernment, we discover how difficult they are. We discover what we see and what we ignore. Our insights are expanded by others. Our fears are triggered. We resist actions where we need to risk. Isn't this complexity always the case with the spiritual life and important decisions? We need a process that is self-correcting and open ended. Yet, we also need a process that leads us to decide and act, rather than circling in indecision.

Remember again the conversation Jesus had with the disciples of John. It is a perfect example of discernment. John's disciples asked Jesus if he was the "anointed one" of God, bringing God's kingdom. He pointed them to actions of healing, of new life, of freedom, and of good news (Luke 7:18-35). Some indeed saw these as the actions of God. They discerned, they judged, and they committed themselves to a vocation and mission of healing, new life, freedom, and good news. But others couldn't see.

How many times do the scriptures talk about people who hear, but do not understand; or those who see and are unable to discern? After the parable of the seeds and the sower, Jesus celebrates those who see and hear: "Happy are your eyes because they see. Happy are your ears because they hear" (Matt 13:16). Many other times he shows his frustration: "Whoever has ears to listen should pay attention!" (Mark 4:9). The conflicts between the many commitments that claim us keep us from seeing. Discernment raises questions of personal faithfulness, corporate responsibility, and participation in the civic aspects of our lives. It is difficult work, potentially conflictual, challenging some of our deepest fears and drawing on some of our deepest commitments.

Therefore, see-judge-act comes with no guarantees. It is but a means, like all of the other models we have seen, to help us in our ongoing search for faithfulness. Being surrounded by a community of persons who are also seeking to be faithful enhances the work.

69

As you engage this process, remember we are discerning together. We bring many different experiences and commitments to our work. See-judge-act calls forth the deepest in us. Therefore, we need communities of openness, mutuality, and care on this journey of discernment. And we also need forgiveness when our discernment lacks focus, when our actions are too weak, and when our judgments are frankly wrong.[6]

See-judge-act is an ongoing, critical, and self-correcting process of seeking to see what God is doing around us and paying attention to what we hear.

Chapter Eleven

The Way of Jesus

Reading for Faithful Living

Jesus was an amazing teacher. He took the ordinary events of people's lives and interpreted them in relationship to his Jewish perspectives and his vision of God's actions in the world. He called scared people to live mutually and restore community. He called sick and broken people to reenter communities as full participating members. He called arrogant, rich people to love God and neighbor.

Jesus also taught with his actions—honoring a woman who touched his robe, acknowledging the thanks of persons he had healed, repenting of dismissing a woman whose daughter was ill, or touching the eyes of a blind man. Jesus embodied the Jewish tradition of loving God and neighbor. He also pointed people to God's amazing actions of healing, freedom, feeding, new life, community, and good news in their midst. He was frustrated when they did not see and particularly when disciples put petty conflicts ahead of gospel. He said, "Pay attention!" (Mark 4:9).

Teaching Biblical Faith Is Teaching the Way of Jesus

This book, *Teaching Biblical Faith*, is about faithfulness—about mission and vocation. The approaches to Bible study we have reviewed seek to connect our faith commitments with life experiences. That was the process embodied in Jesus's teaching, healing, and preaching. As Christians, we follow this way. Writing to those in Rome, calling them brothers and sisters, Paul adds that they are God's adopted children: "But if we are children, we are also heirs. We are God's heirs and fellow heirs with Christ" (Rom 8:17). Writing much later, the author of 1 Peter wrote to his fellow believers, "But you are a chosen race, a royal priesthood, a holy nation, a people who are God's own possession. . . . Once you weren't a people, but now you are God's people" (1 Pet 2:9-10). We are indeed heirs of God and children of God called to follow Jesus. How do we do that? Again, only with purposeful study do we focus our lives on following the way of Jesus. Small group Bible study is one intentional way we can pay attention.

To study and teach the way of Jesus means to "pay attention," and to "dress" ourselves in Jesus—to follow Jesus by embodying what Jesus did.

In another book, *Teaching the Way of Jesus*, I sought to ask specifically what it means to live and teach the way of Jesus.[1] Six crucial features emerged:

1. loving God and neighbor

2. living in God's grace

3. looking for the realm of God

4. calling people to the banquet table

5. resisting the time of trial

6. proclaiming the resurrected one[2]

Love God and Neighbor

At the core of the Jewish tradition is the Shema, a prayer recited every morning and every evening as well as every Sabbath and holy day.[3] Jesus recited it often: "Israel, listen! Our God is the LORD! Only the LORD! Love the LORD your God with all your heart, all your being, and all your strength" (Deut 6:4-5). This prayer led Jesus to remind all he met that loving God and neighbor was their vocation—their responsibility (Matt 22:34-40; Mark 12:28-32; Luke 10:25-28).

Living in God's Grace

For Jesus, God's amazing grace was all around. It allowed the seed that had been spread to yield much fruit at harvest (Mark 4:1-20). It was seen in the amazing bounty of the world and in God's care for all creatures. God's grace healed the sick, forgave sinners, and gave new life to those cast from the community. Jesus lived in God's grace and Jesus pointed others to it.

Looking for the Realm of God

Jesus's first sermon announced the realm of God; his parables focused hearers on the amazing presence of God in their midst (see Mark 1:14-15 and 4:10-34). As we have seen before, Jesus pointed people to acts of healing, freedom, restoring community, and new life. The good news of the gospel was that God's realm was already present—was ubiquitous.

Calling People to the Banquet Table

The image of the banquet table also filled Jesus's teaching. He challenged the traditional practices that rewarded places of honor and status. He opened the table to persons who were usually excluded (Luke 14:14-24), himself eating with outcasts and inviting them into the community (Mark 2:15-17). The banquet table became a symbol for God's inclusive realm, a sacred space where God invited those whom society and culture demeaned to sit in places of honor.

Resisting the Time of Trial

In the prayer Jesus taught the disciples, he petitioned, "And do not bring us to the time of trial" (Luke 11:4 NRSV). The world in which Jesus lived was filled with trials—the oppression of the Romans and the consequences of resistance. Lives were fragile and at risk as persons lost lands and were terrorized by Roman might. Jesus helped people in the villages find ways of living together, sharing, and celebrating even in this atmosphere of state terrorism.

Proclaiming the Resurrected One

Proclaiming new life was what Jesus did and what he called his disciples to do, too. Where there was death, there is now new life and hope. The disciples of John asked Jesus if he was God's anointed one. He, in turn, pointed to them to the markers of the realm of God: healing, freeing, new life, and gospel. The same is true when he sent his disciples out. They were to point to new life—healing bodies, exorcising demonic forces, and offering new life. Paul calls us to clothe ourselves in Christ, so that we indeed proclaim new life as he did: "Dress yourself with the Lord Jesus Christ" (Rom 13:14). Therefore to study and teach the way of Jesus means to "pay attention" and to "dress" ourselves in Jesus— to follow Jesus by embodying what Jesus did.

The Way of Jesus Approach to Teaching

This approach pushes us to ask ourselves how we are being called to live out the ways of Jesus. How do we love God and neighbor, live in God's grace, look for the realm of God, call people to the banquet table, resist the time of trial, and proclaim the resurrected one?

Moreover, as we study the New Testament, we look for the markers of the way of Jesus. We look for the ways the early followers of Jesus understood and sought to live his way. As we study the Hebrew Bible, we remember that this rich tradition formed a people and also formed Jesus. We look at how it shaped him and he drew on it.

We ask how we are faithfully living the way of Jesus.

1. **Begin with prayer**—Honestly ask God to help us pay attention and "dress" ourselves in Jesus so that we are embodying what it means to be followers, to be disciples.

2. **Study the text with integrity**—As we have learned above, study the texts with all of the historical, literary, theological, and spiritual resources we have. Honor the texts for their commitments and meanings.

3. **Furthermore, ask the texts how they help us know Jesus or the community that formed him**—As noted above, when viewing the Gospels and writings, ask where the six elements of the way of Jesus are apparent and how they are communicated and lived. When studying the Hebrew Bible, also think how this rich, diverse tradition was a foundation on which Jesus drew for his way.

4. **Move to our present**—As Jesus asked the hearers to "pay attention," we then pay attention to the way of Jesus. How does this text help us understand how to

   • love God and neighbor,

   • live in God's grace,

- look for the realm of God,

- call people to the banquet table,

- resist the time of trial, and

- proclaim the resurrected one?

5. **Focus on one or two of your conclusions**—As you study and discuss, ask if one or two of your insights claims your attention. Decide where to focus. Ask how you are seeing God's action in the world. Ask how you are following Jesus. Think specifically of a call or claim this reflection puts on your life. Share those insights and commitments in the group. Question and support each other.

6. **Again, be specific and strategic**—Think about next steps, about further reflection needed. Ask who can help you in this journey and in these commitments.

7. **Close with prayer**—First, remind yourselves that you are seeking to live the way of Jesus. Second, thank God for the continuing miracles of new life. Third, ask for support as you seek to live the way of Jesus.

Contributions of the Way of Jesus Approach to Bible Study

Discernment of faithfulness is the task of this approach. To be Christian is to seek the way of Jesus and God's realm to which he pointed. As we saw in the last chapter, acts of discernment are difficult. When we put our lives and commitments in light of the way of Jesus, we feel like the original disciples who quibbled over small things and missed the big things. We hear Jesus's words to them: "Pay attention." Yes, we discover what we attend to and what we ignore. Fears are triggered. We know we resist actions where we need to risk. Moreover, we know that what is true of us is even more true for the community of faith—the church has not always been faithful and will often fail.

But more than this, we know that the way of Jesus had a profound effect on his followers, fundamentally transforming their lives and commitments. Those followers took the gospel into the world proclaiming healing, freedom, new life, and community. They had a transforming effect.

Remember Paul's advice to the community in Corinth, who were divided by status and conflict. He said we see now only in a "glass darkly" (to use the KJV). "Now we see a reflection in a mirror; then we will see face-to-face. Now I know partially, but then I will know completely in the same way that I have been completely known" (1 Cor 13:12). In fact, to use the original Greek, Paul is saying living faithfully is almost a "riddle." We have to work hard, not knowing if the answer will come or make a difference. Yet, even working on the riddle of living or seeing a reflection, Paul affirmed that was enough because we have been "completely known." In other words, we are called with all our limitations and gaps as well as talents and foresight, to seek to "pay attention" and live into God's realm. We won't see all or clearly, but we will see and it will make a difference for those we touch.

A gift of this approach to teaching and study is that it keeps us focused on the way of Jesus. With friends and colleagues, we keep seeking for the way. We pay attention and live as faithfully as we can, hoping for, looking at, and engaging in God's gracious gifts and hopes.

Chapter Twelve

Reading Collegially

Interfaith Reading of Scripture

We live in a world of incredible diversity—diversity of cultures, ethnicities, nationalities, commitments, and even hopes. One significant part of this diversity is religious. We all know religions can shape living for the good. They can attune us to the needs of others. Religions have visions of the common good—of the way life should be and of how we work together for the love and justice of all. We also know that religions also divide. Cultures fight over religious commitments; people are taught to reject those who are different.

A few years ago, I was at an interfaith conference of Jews, Christians and Muslims.[1] We worked hard to hear each other, to respect differences, and to share commitments. At the end of the conference, a young Muslim man stood up and thanked all for their hospitality. He felt welcomed and heard; others agreed. All concluded that interfaith groups sometimes work harder at understanding than groups that share a common faith because they must openly engage differences over theology or institutional commitments and not let them fester.

How do we seek to engage the religious diversity in our local communities? What would it mean for us to study scripture in the midst of others from other faith communities? An example, in Berlin, the Reverend Gregor Hohberg, Rabbi Tovia Ben-Chorin, and Imam Kadir Sanci are building together The House of One, where a church, synagogue, and mosque will use separate congregational facilities in one shared space.[2] Admittedly this may be unusual, yet throughout the world and in our own communities people of diverse faiths touch each other regularly.

Many groups and congregations are planning intentional ways of learning about each other and dealing with misunderstandings.[3] One such example is the Scriptural Reasoning Project, where small groups of persons of different faiths gather together to read each other's scriptures. Their focus is not on consensus, but on understanding and friendship. In fact, their website even offers online helps where people in different locations can actually join in common study.[4]

Another example of a face-to-face project is the work of the Committee on Christian Unity and Interreligious Relationships of the Northern Illinois Conference of the United Methodist Church.[5] For several years, they have offered yearly events for Christians and Muslims. I joined one of these, where we examined two texts—one from the Old Testament and one from the Koran. Both passages attended to the same character and story, yet from very different points of reference. Around tables, we prayed, introduced ourselves, ate together, and in respect and openness shared our understandings. We were careful. We were honest.

As people share across religious traditions, some insights challenge accepted patterns of belief and others confirm them.

Of course, other groups meet much more regularly and for much longer periods of study. They come to experience both the depth of their disagreements as well as their commonalities. The search for meaning and purpose in life is difficult. Religious convictions are some of our deepest, affecting our understandings of our identities and of our callings. As people share across religious traditions, some insights challenge accepted patterns of belief and others confirm them. Therefore, a willingness to share honestly with others the importance of the journey builds respect, even when differences are not bridged.[6]

Interfaith Approach to Teaching and Leading Bible Study

Care, therefore, needs to be taken when entering into teaching and learning sessions with persons of differing faith communities. The Scriptural Reasoning Project offers advice for interfaith groups. The facilitator or convener (or in our words teacher/ animator) is asked to keep in mind and encourage participants to follow four important guidelines:

- keep to the texts

- give space to others' readings

- be open

- be honest[7]

In fact, these are very appropriate rules for any teaching group.

As you begin an interfaith scripture study, the first question to address is what texts to read in common and to study. One approach focuses on texts that are shared across religious traditions: for example, the prophetic books in the Hebrew Bible (Tanakh) are also scripture for Christians, or characters such as Abraham and Sarah are discussed in sacred books of Jewish, Christian, and Muslim traditions. A second option is studying texts on common human themes. Scriptural Reasoning offers examples on its website of sacred texts on topics such as encountering God, wisdom, beginnings, fall, women and equality, education, using God's gifts, and others. A third option is focusing on texts on religious practices: for example, sharing how we pray, celebrate holidays, or care for the sick.[8]

Once texts are chosen, the elements of the interfaith approach to Bible study include the following:

1. **Begin with prayer**—Ask members of each of the religious communities present to offer a prayer for the study. Prayer reminds participants of their commitments and their hopes in the study.

2. **Share with each other what you saw and heard in the texts**—Focus on the texts. Be honest and caring. Describe what you saw happening in the text(s).

3. **Share questions**—Then move to respectful questions of each other. Listen carefully to the answers.

4. **Note commonalities and commitments present in the texts.**

5. **Have a member of each group share some of the historical background and scholarship about the text**—In previous chapters, we have seen the excellent scholarship that is occurring around Christian passages of scripture. The Jewish tradition also has a long history of scholarship beginning in rabbinic interpretations (midrash) and continuing to the present. The same is true of other religious traditions. There are scholarly works as well as histories of interpretation. Ask the friends and colleagues with whom

you are studying to share a resource or two that you might review before gathering again.

6. **Share insights, commitments, and questions that come out of the study**—Be open and honest. Note ongoing questions to which you will attend in further study. The more you study together, the deeper your insights, questions, and commitments will be. The study may also get more difficult as direct disagreements emerge. You will want to ask how these can be respected in a shared world and community. (Again, this concern is also true within each of our religious communities as we deal with people whose views are quite different from our own.) There will be times when you discover "religious" perspectives that all of you will find objectionable—for example, a lack of respect for life or for the communities we seek to build together.

7. **Offer an opportunity for people to share their feelings about the experience of studying together**—Again, be open, honest, and respectful.

8. **Close in prayer**—Have a representative of each community express thanks for the participants, the sharing, the clarifications, and the emerging friendships. Commit to another time to gather, to study, and to learn from each other. (While it may be obvious, a shared meal, shared songs, and shared stories go a long way to build respectful community.)

Contributions of an Interfaith Scripture Reading Approach

What is the result of interfaith study? Or even on a more specific note, what does it mean for us to study texts with people,

Christian and not, who may disagree with us? Dr. Deborah Court of Bar-Ilan University and I have been working on a research project on the reasons for interfaith study. Among our findings were four that are important here.

First, we learn about each other. Since we share this globe together, we need to know who our neighbors are and the commitments that shape them. While this first step may often be shallow and may highlight our differences, it is a value in itself, if we are to share in the common everyday activities of shopping, living, seeking healthcare, and voting.

Second, as we work with others, we encounter the amazing ways all of us religious people share procedures, understandings, and even histories. In fact, conversations about what is at the heart of our differing religious traditions push us to clarify our own traditions and to state their meanings in such a way that others can understand. We learn more about ourselves and the world we share.

Third, since we live together in communities, how decisions are made are important for all of us. When we learn with each other, we find ways we can collaborate in partnership on common projects for the common good. For example, the three great Abrahamic faiths are concerned about "the least of these," historically defined as widows, pilgrims, and strangers. We share a world; together we are concerned about its health.

Learning together deepens our connections to the sources of our own religious traditions.

Fourth, learning together deepens our connections to the sources of our own religious traditions. For example, Christianity is committed to "loving God and neighbors." Jesus learned this in his Jewish upbringing. It is also a principle shared by Islam. When we pray and study with others, we are brought in contact with the deepest of my commitments and with the sources of those commitments—that is, opened to the depth of God's interactions with the world. As Dr. Court says, through interfaith learning, we are opened to spiritual growth. We can no longer be concerned only about our personal spiritual growth. We are enlarged as we seek and recognize our shared connections and insights about creation, community, and future. "How much richer the path might be if our spiritual longings lead us, though study and encounter, to insights about God and meaning offered by various faith traditions."[9]

PART THREE

Advice for Teachers and Leaders

Chapter Thirteen

So I Am a Teacher

Aids for Planning and Leading Bible Study

Whether we have taught many years, a few, or none at all, often the request to teach or lead a congregational Bible study is frightening. We wonder whether we know enough, whether we are faithful enough, whether we can be helpful to others, and whether we can assist a group to address differences or conflicts that may emerge.

Honestly, these feelings are true if you are an experienced teacher or a beginning teacher. We have to consider who we are called to be as teacher-leaders, about the people with whom we are working, and the content and the goals of our teaching.

Thinking about the Teacher-Leader

A concept about teaching that I have found helpful comes out of our discussion of base Christian communities in chapter 9. While many of the people in the neighborhood house churches had limited formal education, they thrived as they studied together as children of God seeking to live fully and faithfully. A powerful definition of the teacher-leader emerged from their lives. A teacher is an *animator*.

What does an animator do? An animator enlivens. The most popular use of the word *animator* comes from the world of cartoon production. An animator envisions a story, draws frames, and gives life to characters. In the base communities, in turn, an animator envisions learning, offers a process, and invites people to make connections for living. A teacher offers life to a group engaged in study. The Bible study leader (animator) honors those who gather offering questions, insights, directions, a listening ear, and a caring space to help people share and grow.

Furthermore, as we know, each student, each member of a teaching/learning community considers the insights and learnings that emerge. The person always connects these to her or his life. Insights come alive, if they seem meaningful and useful. Teachers and leaders do not control learning, rather they invite it; they animate it. They provide occasions that stimulate it. Rather than seeing a teacher as the all-knowing and all-seeing controller of learning, instead teachers and Bible study leaders create a process, honoring the people present, the text, and the insights shared.[1]

Let's look into this process of animating, by considering how to pay attention to the people and to the texts and how to prepare for teaching.

Pay Attention to the People

Who am I "teaching"? Who are the real people that will gather in this Bible study? This is the first question any leader must ask. All teaching and group facilitation begins with *people engaged in study*—whether they are children, youth, young adults, intergenerational groups, senior adults, professional teachers, or even scholars. *Teachers teach people.* Small group leaders help show the way.

Respect, openness, hospitality, and listening are what are required of a teacher and of group Bible study members.

Through small group Bible studies, we gather to grow in faith—to live more fully as faithful people. Therefore, small group Bible studies begin with prayer and sharing of what is happening in people's lives. In turn, I, as a teacher, never enter a classroom without praying for the people that I will meet. The events and experiences of their lives profoundly affect how they hear the content shared and the insights of others. For example, if a dear friend has just died, that loss will be present in any wrestling with texts or engaging in conversation. The same is true of events in our communities that affect our lives—when personal events and illnesses challenge us, when storms damage homes and shut off electricity, or when our brokenness is so blatant in events of racism, school violence, or injustice. The events of our lives shape our study and reflection. Remember, chapters 7, 8, and 9 illustrated ways that personal and cultural experiences connected with learning and offered strategies for teachers to engage these experiences as well.

Furthermore, our backgrounds and previous learning profoundly affects our study. When a group has studied together over a period of time—in a lectionary Bible study, an ongoing in-depth study like DISCIPLE or Covenant—previous learning profoundly shapes its present sharing (see chapters 3, 4, 5, and 6). A group of persons who have been in an ongoing study for a time will have developed a foundation of learning on which they build. Their experience is much different from a group of persons meeting together for the first time or reading the Bible for the first time.

Respect, openness, hospitality, and listening are what

are required of a teacher and of group Bible study members. Connecting the Bible with our personal lives is a profound activity that has consequences. When one reads that God created life and we learn deep in our souls that we are all children of God, we are profoundly grateful for God's grace. When we read Isaiah, Jeremiah, or Amos, learning how "faithful people" can dismiss and abuse our fellows, we recognize that we may not be living up to the goals God has for us. Our own broken relationships and our stereotypes profoundly call for repentance and new ways of living. When we seek to be faithful and struggle and struggle, not knowing what to do or not willing to really do it, we cry out "LORD, . . . you know me" (Ps 139:1).[2]

Small groups of people who can hold each other in love and accountability are rich places of learning—of seeking to be faithful. It is important for groups to be honest about the depth of the teaching/learning process. They must intentionally name that they will receive each other with integrity and respect. Pains will be shared, of course; hopes will be shared; and challenges and differences will emerge. Faithfulness demands we treat each other as children of God.

Small groups of people who can hold each other in love and accountability are rich places of learning—of seeking to be faithful.

Let me suggest a strategy of teaching and group work that can help us in this hard work. United Methodists speak of the method as "holy conferencing"—drawn from John Wesley's efforts to assist small groups to live social holiness. Bishop Sally Dyck has defined the process of holy conferencing in the following principles:

1. Every person is a child of God.

2. Listen before speaking.

3. Strive to understand from another's point of view.

4. Strive to reflect accurately the views of others.

5. Disagree without being disagreeable.

6. Speak about issues; do not defame people.

7. Pray, in silence or aloud, before decisions.

8. Let prayer interrupt your busyness.[3]

She adds, "No wonder that John Wesley said that Christian conferencing is a means of grace, for it puts us in the position of growing in spiritual maturity."[4] I recommend these as "rules" or expectations for study groups. Share them, post them, and talk about them. Indeed, acknowledge the depth and importance of searching the scriptures and seeking to claim our vocations as children of God. Pay attention to each other.

Pay Attention to the Text

Faithfulness is the goal of the teaching/learning process. Scripture is our guide, as it has been for Christian people for generations. Our ancestors have witnessed to us through these texts; they have spoken about how God loves and challenges. They defined ways to build just communities. This process of exploring life in relation to scripture has continued throughout the Christian movement as our forebears sought to understand to whom they were committed and for what they stood. We join it. As noted in chapter 1, faith calls for prayer and humility as well as study and theological reflection to seek to discern God's will.

In our study, scripture passages are interpreted. We consider the purposes of a text's author, the context that shaped the author's work, and the living realities of our present. Preaching and teaching come alive when the words of the biblical text connect to the realities of living in which they were shaped and to current realities of everyday life. For example, Jeremiah shared God's disgust with the people's brokenness and taking advantage of each other. His words were shaped out of actual experiences of the Hebrew people under the threat of Babylonian armies. His words continue to speak to us today because we know the realities of brokenness and threat in our lives. Or another example: the writer of Matthew deeply believed in the revelation brought by Jesus. He lived in a community of great diversity in Antioch. Shaped by great Hebrew traditions, he witnessed to his neighbors about Jesus's connections with Jewish ancestors. Scripture interpretation connects the words of a passage, with its context, and to our present.[5]

Therefore, the teacher/leader/animator asks what the text says, what we know about its author and the realities that shaped this witness, and how it speaks to our time and living. Honestly, that is what the word *scripture* means. *Scripture* is a living witness to God's interactions with community. Yet, scripture must be interpreted. As it is interpreted, differences of opinions and differing insights emerge. That is simply what happens when people work together. The guidelines for teaching offered in chapter 12 help us deal with this natural reality of diverse interpretations:

- keep to the texts

- give space to others' readings

- be open

- be honest[6]

We will want to acknowledge the differing perspectives and disagreements, yet in open and honest dialogue. As we hear one another, we each are testing our own insights in the midst of community. As we share commitments or actions we hope to carry out, we are inviting colleagues to journey with us and ask us, How is it going? How are you living your call from God? Pay attention to the text.

Pay Attention to the Process of Teaching

Basic questions all teachers ask include the following:

- Who are we teaching?

- What will we teach?

- How will we use and enrich the environment for learning?

- How will the teaching/learning session flow?

- On what resources and practices will we draw?

- What do we hope students will learn?[7]

To assist us to answer these questions, I offer the following guide to preparing a teaching/learning session. Consider each step as you plan:

1. **Context**—Pay attention to the learners.

2. **Content**—Pay attention to the text.

3. **Learning goals**—Focus on what you hope people will learn. (Note each of the approaches in chapters 3–12 have specific learning goals.)

4. **Environment**—Attend to space/room. Note what supplies and format you need.

5. **Flow of the teaching**—Think about your time together. Think about how you will begin the session, how it will proceed, and how it will end. (In defining teaching practices, look particularly at the steps of a session defined in chapters 3–12.)

6. **Evaluation**—Think about your time together. Note signs of learning in those in the small group and in yourself. Think about what enhances learning in the group.[8]

Each of the approaches described in chapters 3–12 have a specific flow. Each chapter guides a teacher in preparing—in how to begin, shape, and end a teaching and learning session. Yet beyond these processes, a teacher pays attention to the people and the environment for learning deciding what needs to be added—for example, perhaps discussing the method of "holy conferencing" or the ways the group interacts. The teacher/animator always asks himself or herself, as well as the group, How is our life together? What is helping us grow in faith? Ask these questions in the spirit of prayer, knowing God is present in your midst. Pay attention to the process of teaching and learning.

Conclusion

To understand the power of teaching, Dean Mary Elizabeth Mullino Moore of Boston University has offered a profound and beautiful image—*teaching is "from the heart."*[9] What she means is that teaching touches the rhythms of life. Teaching moves from one heart to another as we receive life, support, and hope from each other. Through teaching and learning, we share our convictions—what animates us and gives us life as people and a community.

Begin in prayer, know God is present, pay attention to yourself as teacher and to the group, pay attention to the text, and pay attention to the teaching-learning process. Trust that you together can indeed glimpse God's grace and hope for living.

Chapter Fourteen

Shaping a Biblical Congregation

Bible study in small groups helps parishioners grow in knowledge of the faith, claim their identities as Christian persons, and live their vocations as followers of Jesus. Bible study is the key place where persons connect faith to living.

This chapter is directed to members of church education committees, church boards, teachers, pastors, and directors of education. It addresses how we can assist those with whom we serve, work, and worship to know themselves as children of God, to encounter God's vision of shalom for all the world, and to follow God into abundant living—to embody biblical faith. We can create rich and powerful teaching ministries that make a difference in people's lives.

Amidst discordant voices of our time, failures and outright injustices, and many competing perspectives, we need attention and study to help us live as followers of Jesus. As we discussed in chapter 1, living biblical faith means that a person seeks to embody the commitments set forth in the tradition to love God and neighbor, to touch the distressed with mercy and justice, and to gain the practical wisdom to see and follow God's realm. This is redemptive living. For us to be able to live redemptively, we need to study the scriptures deeply, using all of the resources at hand, in a community of friends and colleagues who seek with us and hold us accountable.

The approaches we have studied offer us direction. They have helped us

- understand the texts of scripture;

- consider the purposes and commitments of the authors of the scriptures;

- explore theological themes;

- pray with scripture;

- engage our stories, cultures, and experiences;

- define options for mission and vocation;

- discuss faith and public life with persons of other faith traditions; and

- follow the way of Jesus.

While I know that groups studying this book have probably only explored some of its methods, they have sparked their hunger for sustained, systematic, theological, and biblical reflection to grow in faith and wisdom.

We need attention and study to help us live as followers of Jesus.

Let's now turn to ways of enhancing teaching for biblical faith. In chapter 2, the educational practices that shaped Jesus and his followers were defined as

1. regular worship (*Shabbat*) with its prayers and study of Torah (Law) and Prophets,

2. annual celebrations to remember the gifts of God,

3. ongoing daily study, and

4. furthermore, Jesus's own calling of people to follow the markers of the realm of God (mission).

Today, excellent Christian education ministries continue this pattern. They are comprehensive, connecting worship, rituals of faith, study, and mission. Let's explore each.

Worship

Sunday worship is the regular Christian practice for which churches are known. Through it, we celebrate God's gifts and the new life God offered the world through Jesus. Just as in Jesus's time, and that of his followers, at the heart of worship is interpreting the scriptures in light of everyday experiences and meanings.

Each Sabbath, Jesus would attend synagogue to listen to interpretations of Torah and the Prophets connected to the realities of people's lives. Synagogue worship sought to name and define how people were to live. Moreover, each morning and evening, faithful people would repeat the Shema prayer to remind them that God is, that God the creator deserves love and trust, and that God calls them to love and guard their neighbors.

As texts were heard, prayers repeated, and interpretations given, people focused on how they were to live. In fact, the very act of interpretation, connecting a text to its context and to its present, called people to faithfulness. For example, hearing that God had sent Jonah to the strangers in Nineveh, even when Jonah didn't want to go, meant that God was sending people to proclaim God's care and gifts to strangers.

Jesus's followers continued this practice of interpreting the Law and Prophets. To it, they added emerging letters from Christian leaders and the Gospels, which reminded them of the acts and expectations of Jesus. In fact, these letters and Gospels were in themselves forms of interpretation. For example, Paul attended to real events in real communities—questions about death in Thessalonians and conflicts in Corinth. He interpreted what they should do in light of his faith in and experience of the risen one. Another example: the writer of Luke took the events he had heard of the life of Jesus and interpreted them for new communities. "Many people have already applied themselves to the task of compiling an account of the events that have been fulfilled among us. They used what the original eyewitnesses and servants of the word handed down to us. Now, after having investigated everything carefully from the beginning, I have also decided to write a carefully ordered account for you" (Luke 1:1-3). He continued this process of connecting the past to the present in the book of Acts. As he shared the journeys of the followers of Jesus, he showed how the people of God could follow the realm of God in concrete events of daily living.

Each Sunday, scripture is interpreted in light of its context and our living context in the world. We learn through prayers, hymns, and sermons. Make those moments rich and empowering for living. Relate them to the real lives of people in the congregation. One way to enhance this process is an ongoing lectionary study group (chapter 6). Here the people of God participate with worship leaders in considering texts and their interpretation. Together they connect faith with life.

Seasonal Festivals of Faith

In Jesus's world there were rich celebrations: weekly Sabbath and yearly events such as Passover, *Shavuot*, and *Sukkot*. Through celebrating Passover, people remembered God's actions to free them—to covenant with them and to empower them to be witnesses of God's grace. Through *Shavuot*, the people remembered God's commandments that defined them and bound them as a people. The commandments were not burdens, but gifts helping them to embody God's expectations. *Sukkot* reminded the people of their total dependence on God. While wandering in the wilderness, they would have died without God's care—a guiding "pillar of fire" and food (manna).

In a similar fashion today, the regular seasons of the church year point to the meanings of being Christian: Advent, expectation; Epiphany, presence; Lent, penitence; and Easter, new life. The rhythm of the year reminds us of the rhythms of our lives. Through our celebration of these seasons, we explicitly connect stories of faith with the realities of the world.

Make these celebrations rich and eventful. Take every opportunity to interpret their meanings. Offer small groups that explore their rhythms and implications. Connect these studies with worship and congregational planning.

Ongoing Study

Let me share the educational ministry of one church as an example. This congregation developed a systematic curriculum of study that begins with five foundational courses (all four to six weeks):

- Beginning Biblical Study,

- Exploring the Old Testament,

- Exploring the New Testament,

- Living Faithfully: The Theological Story, and

- Living the Faith in Daily Life.

Members, particularly new members, are reminded to complete all of these courses as foundations for further study. Therefore, systematic scripture study begins with learning exegetical processes (chapter 3). It continues as people become acquainted with the key themes and stories of the Old and New Testaments (remember the "worry" and "hunger" described in the introduction). Then it expands as people explore the ongoing theological tradition and faithful reflection in daily life.

Building on the foundational studies, this faith community schedules other elective experiences. In the last two years, this church has offered classes on praying the scriptures, looking at the Psalms and each Gospel (chapter 7); on books of the Bible, looking at the Prophets (chapter 4); regular thematic studies using DISCIPLE and Covenant (chapter 5); an ongoing lectionary group (chapter 6); and small groups reflecting on events of daily work life (chapter 9). They have even sponsored for a month an interfaith study with a local mosque (chapter 12).

Study is crucial to ongoing growth in faith. Most of the approaches described in this book are appropriate for both ongoing and short-term studies, whether on Sunday or throughout the week. Simply pick some and try them. See how they enhance the ways you connect text, our friends and colleagues in the faith, our histories and cultures, and our commitments as Christian persons and witnesses to God's grace.

Following Jesus

Jesus brought new life and hope to his time. The pain of oppression and the power of the Roman authorities had limited people's options. Jesus pointed to the realm of God powerfully present in the healing of the sick, the forgiving and restoring of those who had sinned, the proclaiming of release to prisoners burdened with oppression and debt, the offering of good news to the poor, and the restoring of community. His vision was concrete. For Jesus these acts both occurred in his present and would be more fully fulfilled in the future. Jesus called followers to work to make this good news into actual realities.

Teaching biblical faith requires, as we have discussed, ongoing study, the support of friends and colleagues, and the engagement of everyday living with God's good news. Thus to be faithful to the vision of Jesus, we, his followers, add to our worship and ongoing study intentional reflection on mission in the world. The processes of see-judge-act (chapter 10) and living the way of Jesus (chapter 11) can empower every task force and program area of a congregation. Intentionally and thoroughly, they should ask, To what is God calling us? Where are we seeing and following God's realm into the world?

The goal of teaching biblical faith is living biblical faith.

Moreover, these are precisely the questions that should be asked as we plan the ministries of congregations. While faith communities provide support, care, and education for members, these congregations also carry the way of Jesus into the wider world. Intentionally and purposefully, the same strategies of biblical education and faithful theological reflection (chapters 10 and 11) become processes of planning and empowerment—educating and leading congregations to "see" the realm of God in their communities, to "judge" how they will embody God's call, and to "enact" ministries of faithfulness. Just as congregations guide members to live the way of Jesus, faithful congregations incarnate the way of Jesus.

Living Biblical Faith

Study is powerful, it is rewarding, and it gives meaning to our living, yet its purpose is faithfulness. The goal of teaching biblical faith is thus living biblical faith. Where indeed are we healing the sick, forgiving and restoring those who have sinned, proclaiming release and new life to prisoners, offering the good news to all, and restoring community?

We are followers of Jesus; that is our identity. Seeing as Jesus saw and hoping as Jesus hoped, we experience the abundance that offers mercy and care for those who are suffering and victims of the systemic evils of our world. Our mission is living biblical faith. May God's vision become so clear that we indeed follow Jesus and love God and neighbors!

Select Resources for a Church's Study Library

These resources assist a congregation to support teaching and learning biblical faith.

Study Bibles

Study Bibles reproduce a translation of the biblical text as well as include articles on general issues in biblical study, introductions to each book describing the views of scholars on authorship and context, concordances (indexes of biblical terms), and maps. Churches should provide two or three excellent study Bibles.

Some of the best options are the Common English Bible (CEB), the New Revised Standard Version (NRSV), and the New International Version (NIV). All reflect current scholarship. Most people consider the NRSV to represent more mainline progressive scholarship while the NIV reflects more conservative scholarship. The CEB is the newest translation—with an ecumenical editorial board made up of representatives from many denominations and including more women translators than any other Bible currently available.

I also recommend a Jewish study Bible. One can then consider the differences of interpretation in the Jewish community and the Christian community about the Hebrew Bible—the Old

Testament. In addition, an outstanding Jewish annotated commentary on the New Testament appropriately sets the discussion of New Testament books in their Jewish and Roman context.

You will find online translations of the Bible where differing texts can be viewed; for example, one of the best is BibleGateway. com. You will also find apps for digital devices.

- *The CEB Study Bible with Apocrypha.* Joel B. Green, general editor. Nashville: Common English Bible, 2013.

- *NIV Study Bible.* Grand Rapids: Zondervan, 2014.

- *HarperCollins Study Bible: New Revised Standard Version (with the Apocryphal/Deuterocanonical Books).* Wayne A. Meeks, general editor. New York: Harper Collins, 1993. (New version has Harold Attridge as general editor and is from 2006.)

- *The Jewish Study Bible: Featuring the Jewish Publication Society TANAKH Translation.* Oxford: Oxford University Press, 2004.

- *The Jewish Annotated New Testament. New Revised Standard Version Translation.* Amy-Jill Levine and Marc Zvi Brettler, editors. Oxford: Oxford University Press, 2011.

Bible Concordance

A concordance is simply an index to the biblical text. Each of the main translations will have their own index/concordance. This tool assists a student in finding particular words or phrases used in the text. Online searching can be better than a concordance (concordances tend to be keyed to English words, not the original Hebrew and Greek).

- *Common English Bible: Concise Concordance.* Nashville: Common English Bible, 2013

- *The Concise Concordance to the New Revised Standard Version.* John R. Kohlenberger, III, editor. Oxford: Oxford University Press, 1993.

- *NIV Bible Concordance.* John R. Kohlenberger, III, editor. Reissue edition. Grand Rapids: Zondervan, 2012.

- *Tanakh Plus with Concordance and Gematria.* CD-ROM. Scottsdale, AZ: Hebrew World Distribution, 2013.

Bible Dictionary

A Bible dictionary discusses ideas, names, words, places, and books appearing in the Bible. Some Bible dictionaries include maps. While there are many Bible dictionaries, some are comprehensive and others abbreviated. The first two listed below are one-volume dictionaries; the last two are multivolume sets.

- *The Common English Bible: Bible Dictionary.* Nashville: Common English Bible, 2011.

- *Eerdmans Dictionary of the Bible.* David Noel Freeman, editor. Grand Rapids: Eerdmans, 2000.

- *The New Interpreters Dictionary of the Bible.* Katharine Doob Sakenfeld, editor. Nashville: Abingdon Press, 2009.

- *Anchor Bible Dictionary.* David Noel Freedman, editor. New Haven, CT: Yale University Press, 1992.

Bible Maps

A set of useable classroom maps assists students in understanding the land of Palestine and the early church as well as the relationship among cities and towns in differing eras. A fine set of maps that is comprehensive, easily understood, and able to be stored on library shelves is the *Bible Map Guide*. National Geographic produces these maps. You will find other Bible maps online.

- *Common English Bible: Bible Map Guide; Explore the Lands of the Old and New Testament.* Nashville: Common English Bible, 2011.

Commentaries and Books

There are many outstanding commentaries on biblical books. A commentary moves verse by verse in analyzing the meaning, history, and context of biblical verses and passages. In addition, many outstanding publications and scholarly journals on biblical times and biblical concepts are being published. They reflect multiple theological and faith tradition perspectives as well as many cultural perspectives. I recommend each church decide on some key resource books to enhance study.

The Society for Biblical Literature is the primary scholarly association of biblical scholars. Its website is www.sbl-site.org. The site includes scholarly resources for biblical study as well as discussion of the teaching of the Bible in public schools.

Notes

Introduction: Bible Study Matters

1. See Margaret Ann Crain and Jack L. Seymour, *Yearning for God: Reflections of Faithful Lives* (Nashville: Upper Room Books, 2003).

2. Jack Seymour, *Teaching the Way of Jesus* (Nashville: Abingdon Press, 2014), 58.

3. For a fuller discussion of this process, see ibid., 101–3.

1. Biblical Faith

1. For an approach to theological reflection, see Seymour, *Teaching the Way of Jesus*, 55–61.

2. Walter Brueggemann, *Creative Word: Canon as a Model for Biblical Education* (Philadelphia: Fortress Press, 1982).

3. Ibid., 15.

4. In Jesus's day, the Torah was read, as it is in synagogues today, in sections from beginning to end, in one year, so that the people are reminded of the identity and vocation given by God.

5. The whole text of the Shema consists of Deut 6:4-9; 11:13-21; and Num 15:37-41. To understand this passage, also see Lev 19:15-18. Jewish faithful still pray the Shema each morning and evening so that they focus living on God. In fact, the golden rule is drawn from the work of Hillel, who preceded Christianity. He is quoted as saying, "What is hateful to you, do not to your neighbour: that is the whole Torah, while the rest is the commentary thereof; go and learn it" (Babylonian Talmud, *Shabbath* 31a).

6. See Seymour, *Teaching the Way of Jesus*, 132–33.

2. Teaching Biblical Faith

1. For a fuller description of this process, see chapters 4–6 in Seymour, *Teaching the Way of Jesus.*

2. In fact, studying the Torah is itself understood as such a gracious gift of God that each Sabbath, even today, as the Torah is removed from the Holy Ark, people dance in joy. Studying the Torah defines the relationship to God.

3. While collections of writings were being assembled as early as 150 CE, the final form of what we know as the Christian Bible was formally defined between the second and fourth centuries. Daniel Reid states a fine description of this process: "The NT we know today took shape as it bubbled up from the broad-based spiritual wisdom, insight, and devotion of the church. The books selected to be in the NT impressed themselves on the church and were so received as scripture and then accepted as canonical" (Daniel Reid, "How We Got the Bible," in *The CEB Study Bible with Apocrypha* [Nashville: Common English Bible, 2013], 543). See also Michael Greenwald, "The Canon of the New Testament," in *The Jewish Annotated New Testament*, ed. Amy-Jill Levine and Marc Zvi Brettler (Oxford University Press, 2011), 257–60.

4. See "The Wesleyan Means of Grace," The United Methodist Church, http://www.umc.org/how-we-serve/the-wesleyan-means-of-grace.

5. See Seymour, *Teaching the Way of Jesus*, 132–33.

3. Historical (Exegetical) Study

1. For example, see *The CEB Study Bible with Apocrypha*, 4–11. The discussion of the two creation stories and their intent and authorship is fulsome. It also includes a fine discussion of gender and translation (see p. 10). See also *CEB Bible Dictionary* (Nashville: Common English Bible, 2011).

2. At the end of the book, I provide a more complete listing of resources. Most of the major contemporary translations of the Bible can be purchased in a study Bible format. The Common English Bible is the one I am using here for biblical quotations. Two other important study Bibles are the New Revised Standard Version and New International Version. A good church library should have several study Bibles.

3. There are references to biblical concepts and passages on the World Wide Web. Simply use a search engine, asking for a passage. You will get references from biblical quotations to sermons to scholarly articles to Wikipedia summaries. Many of these are helpful; others are not. While I do not discourage

you from using the web, I encourage you to trust more the accepted study Bibles and Bible dictionaries. They have been vetted and represent the best scholarship.

4. This last step is what scholars call *hermeneutics*, meaning a method of interpretation. It is extending the meaning of a text from its own time into our time. For example, when I read letters that my father wrote to my mother during his military service in WWII, I know these are letters between two recently married persons who were separated. The events my dad describes are affected by his desire to share with my mom but also to spare her worry and pain. They provide important historical data but are affected by his purposes. Their meaning can be extended into my present, as I saw my parents interacting with love and seeking to raise my brother and me with certain values.

4. Book-by-Book Studies

1. See chapter 1 and the discussion of Brueggemann's concepts of priestly, prophetic, and wisdom faith.

2. See the conclusion of this book, where I describe select resources for a church's study library. Included are study Bibles and Bible dictionaries.

5. Living the Themes of Faith

1. Again, look at the list of select resources at the end of this book.

2. See Elaine Graham's discussion of apologetics in *Between a Rock and a Hard Place: Public Theology in a Post-Secular Age* (London: SCM Press, 2013). Graham notes that early Christian apologists pointed to the ways Christians lived and loved neighbors as an example of the truth of their convictions (see chapter 6, "Jews, Pagans, Skeptics and Emperors: Public Theology as Christian Apologetics"). See also the similar argument made in Rodney Stark, *The Rise of Christianity: How the Obscure, Marginal Jesus Movement Became the Dominant Religious Force in the Western World in a Few Centuries* (San Francisco: HarperSanFrancisco, 1997).

3. See the discussion of these markers in chapter 1 and also in Seymour, *Teaching the Way of Jesus*, 132–33.

6. Lectionary Studies

1. For an accessible discussion of the lectionary, see "What is the Revised Common Lectionary?," The Revised Common Lectionary, http://lectionary.library.vanderbilt.edu/faq2.php.

2. For the websites of these curricular resources, see http://www.cokesbury.com/ for The United Methodist Church curriculum publishing; http://wearesparkhouse.org/, a division of the Evangelical Lutheran Church; http://www.wholepeopleofgod.com/, an ecumenical Canadian publishing house; or http://www.feastingontheword.net/, a project of Westminster John Knox Press affiliated with the Presbyterian Church (USA) that provides a full set of lectionary worship and commentary resources as well as the curriculum.

3. For example, The United Methodist Board of Discipleship provides a website with lectionary resources. See "Worship Planning," General Board of Discipleship, http://www.gbod.org/worship/worship-planning.

4. For a description of narrative lectionary in relationship to *The Revised Common Lectionary*, see Luther Seminary, Working Preacher, https://www.workingpreacher.org.

5. See the discussion of the steps of theological reflection and meaning making in the lives of ordinary believers on pp. xv–xvi.

6. In contrast, Jewish patterns of worship move in fifty-four weeks sequentially through the passages (*parashah*) of the Torah. This pattern dates from early centuries BCE. Developers also determined prophetic books (*haphtarah*) and Psalms to read alongside the Torah texts.

7. Praying the Scriptures

1. Thomas Merton, quoted on at "Retreat Information," Abbey of Gethsemani, http://www.monks.org/index.php/visit-us/retreats.

2. For a discussion of these dynamics of praying scripture see, Jack L. Seymour, *Praying the Gospel of Mark: On Faith and Blindness* (Nashville: Upper Room Books, 1988), 9–14, 64–70. See also Walter Brueggemann, *Praying the Psalms: Engaging Scripture and the Life of the Spirit*, 2nd ed. (Eugene, OR: Wipf & Stock, 2007).

3. William Thompson, *The Gospels for Your Whole Life: Mark and John in Prayer and Study* (Minneapolis: Winston Press, 1983).

4. Yet, remember, you are free to use the ongoing process of *lectio divina* or Thompson's process—all are efforts to pray the scriptures.

8. Story and Scripture

1. Anne Streaty Wimberly, *Soul Stories: African American Christian Education*, rev. ed. (Nashville: Abingdon Press, 2005).

2. Ibid., 24–26.

3. Ibid., 29.

4. For an overview of the approach, see ibid., 39–48.

9. Theology for Daily Living

1. See Robert O'Gorman, "Latin American Theology and Education," in *Theological Approaches to Christian Education*, ed. Jack L. Seymour and Donald Miller (Nashville: Abingdon Press, 1990), 195–215. Following the work of Vatican II with its focus on empowering the people of God, particularly the poor, base communities expanded, becoming places of worship, hope, service, and renewal. A fuller description of base communities is given in Gustavo Gutierrez, *A Theology of Liberation: History, Politics and Salvation*, rev. ed. (Maryknoll, NY: Orbis Books, 1988); and Michael Griffin and Jennie Weiss Block, eds., *In the Company of the Poor: Conversations with Dr. Paul Farmer and Fr. Gustavo Gutierrez* (Maryknoll, NY: Orbis Books, 2013).

2. Robert O'Gorman, "The Faith Community," in *Mapping Christian Education: Approaches to Congregational Learning*, ed. Jack L. Seymour (Nashville: Abingdon Press, 1997), 47.

3. See the one-volume edition: Ernesto Cardenal, *The Gospel in Solentiname*, trans. Donald D. Walsh (Maryknoll, NY: Orbis Books, 2010).

4. See Ernesto Cardenal, *The Gospel in Solentiname*, trans. Donald D. Walsh, vol. 4 (Maryknoll, NY: Orbis Books, 1982), 61–69.

5. Rita Halteman Finger, *Roman House Churches for Today: A Practical Guide for Small Groups* (Grand Rapids: Eerdmans, 2007); and Robert Jewett, *Romans: A Commentary*, Hermeneia (Minneapolis: Fortress Press, 2006).

6. See Rodney Stark, *Cities of God: The Real Story of How Christianity Became an Urban Movement and Conquered Rome*, repr. ed. (New York: HarperOne, 2007).

7. Remember the process of meaning discovery defined in the introduction. Look back on the pattern. Note this process describes what happens in the theology at sunset approach. Do consider how this process of meaning discovery is occurring in your teaching and learning groups. Check with participants. Are we assisting people as they move naturally through the steps? Are we

allowing for clarity about issues and concerns, are we exploring texts sufficiently, are we moving to decisions, and are we holding each other accountable?

10. See-Judge-Act

1. See the website of the Young Christian Workers: http://www.cijoc.org/. See also the website of the Cardijn Community for the history of Cardinal Cardijn and the method: http://www.cardijncommunity.org. Fr. Cardijn later became a bishop and cardinal.

2. Pope John XXIII, "*Mater et Magistra*: Encyclical of Pope John XXXIII on Christianity and Social Progress," May 15, 1961. The encyclical is available online at both the Vatican website and papal encyclicals website: http://www.vatican.va/holy_father/john_xxiii/encyclicals/documents/hf_j-xxiii_enc_15051961_mater_en.html, and http://www.papalencyclicals.net/John23/j23mater.htm.

3. *The National Plan for Hispanic/Latino Ministry of The United Methodist Church, 2013–2016 Quadrennium Booklet* (New York: National Plan for Hispanic/Latino Ministry, 2013), 8.

4. For other examples of approaches to faithful discernment, see Luke Timothy Johnson, *Scripture and Discernment: Decision Making in the Church* (Nashville: Abingdon Press, 1996); and Danny E. Morris and Charles M. Olsen, *Discerning God's Will Together: A Spiritual Practice for the Church*, rev. and updated ed. (Herndon, VA: Alban Institute, 2012).

5. Note I am adapting the questions suggested by the Young Christian Workers of Australia website: http://www.ycw.org.au/seejudgeact.php. Quotations in the numbered list are drawn from the process on the website.

6. Look at the suggestions about working together in learning communities in chapter 13. Particularly look at the process of holy conferencing suggested for The United Methodist Church.

11. The Way of Jesus

1. For the method used to discern these emphases, see Seymour, *Teaching the Way of Jesus*, 148–50.

2. Ibid., 150. While I will give a summary of these here, see the full description in chapter 7 of ibid., 145–59.

3. The *Shema Y'Israel* includes Deut 6:4-9; 11:13-21; and Num 15:37-41. The meaning of the prayer is extend in Lev 19:18, "You must love your neighbor as yourself; I am the LORD" and the Ten Commandments.

12. Reading Collegially

1. See Hanan A. Alexander and Ayman K. Agbaria, eds. *Commitment, Character, and Citizenship: Religious Education in Liberal Democracy* (New York: Routledge, 2012).

2. See the website of the effort for The House of One, http://house-of -one.org/en. While this story has been published in many places, also see the brief article on it in the *Huffington Post* on June 14, 2014 by Yasmine Hafiz, "Berlin Plans 'House of One,' A Place Where Jews, Muslims, and Christians Will Pray under the Same Roof," http://www.huffingtonpost.com/2014/06/14 /house-of-one-berlin-interfaith_n_5489444.html. See also a longer article, Michael Scaturro, "An Imam, a Rabbi, a Pastor, and the Legacy of a Nazi Church," *The Atlantic*, October 21, 2013, http://www.theatlantic.com/inter national/archive/2013/10/an-imam-a-rabbi-a-pastor-and-the-legacy-of-a-nazi -church/280703/?single_page=true.

3. See, for example, Sheryl Kujawa-Holbrook, *God beyond Borders: Interreligious Learning among Faith Communities* (Eugene, OR: Cascade, 2014); Mary C. Boys, Sara Lee, and Dorothy Bass, *Christians & Jews in Dialogue: Learning in the Presence of the Other* (Woodstock, VT: SkyLight Paths, 2008); and Scriptural Reasoning, Cambridge Inter-faith Programme, http://www .scripturalreasoning.org/.

4. See Scriptural Reasoning, "Scriptural Reasoning Goes Virtual," Cambridge Inter-faith Programme, http://www.scripturalreasoning.org/scriptural -reasoning-goes-virtual.

5. See Northern Illinois Conference of The United Methodist Church, "Christian Unity," http://www.umcnic.org/ministries/outreach/christian -unity/.

6. For the power of such an ongoing group, see Ranya Idliby, Suzanne Oliver, and Priscilla Warner, *The Faith Club: A Muslim, a Christian, a Jew— Three Women Search for Understanding* (New York: Free Press, 2006).

7. See the fuller description of these guidelines on Scriptural Reasoning, "Guidelines for Scriptural Reasoning," Cambridge Inter-faith Programme, http://www.scripturalreasoning.org/guidelines-scriptural-reasoning.

8. See Boys, Lee and Bass, *Christians & Jews in Dialogue*.

9. See Deborah Court and Jack Seymour, "What Might Meaningful Interfaith Education Look Like? Exploring Politics, Principles and Pedagogy," *Religious Education* 110 (October/December, 2015).

13. So I Am a Teacher

1. There are many resources to assist with the process of teaching. One is to contact your congregation's pastor or educator and ask for assistance. Many denominations provide online resources: (1) The United Methodist Church, "Leadership Resources," General Board of Discipleship, http://www.gbod .org/leadership-resources; (2) the Presbyterian Church (USA), "Educational Ministries," Presbyterian Mission Agency, http://www.presbyterianmission .org/ministries/education/; or (3) the ecumenical Faith Formation Learning Exchange, Vibrant Faith, http://www.faithformationlearningexchange.net/. Most local denominational offices also provide assistance for teacher training and teacher resources. In addition to online resources, I recommend to you the writings of Delia Halverson and Barbara Bruce. Also, most comprehensive, thematic Bible studies provide online resources for teachers; see, for example, "Tools for Group Leaders," Covenant Bible Study, http://www.covenant biblestudy.com/Lead-a-Group.

2. Look at chapter 7 on praying the scriptures and chapter 10 on the see-judge-act method to see how study connects to mission and vocation. Remember the conversation in the introduction about the concerns that call the people of God to draw on the resources of their faith to engage everyday living. See Crain and Seymour, *Yearning for God*.

3. Sally Dyck, *Eight Principles of Holy Conferencing: A Study Guide for Churches and Groups* (Minnesota Annual Conference, 2012), 3–14. See also United Church of Christ, "Tips for Faithful and Respectful Discussion," http://www.ucc.org/ourfaithourvote/discussion.html, which has been used in Lutheran, Presbyterian, and United Church of Christ denominational meetings.

4. Dyck, *Eight Principles of Holy Conferencing*, 15.

5. An excellent summary of the process of interpretation is Stephen Garfinkel, "Conservative Jewish Interpretation," in *The Oxford Encyclopedia of Biblical Interpretation*, ed. Stephen L. McKenzie (New York: Oxford University Press, 2013), 131–38. See also Walter Brueggemann, William Placher, and Brian Blount, *Struggling with Scripture* (Louisville: Westminster John Knox, 2002).

6. See the fuller description of these guidelines on Scriptural Reasoning, "Guidelines for Scriptural Reasoning," Cambridge Inter-faith Programme, http://www.scripturalreasoning.org/guidelines-scriptural-reasoning.

7. Revised from Seymour, *Teaching the Way of Jesus*, 104.

8. Revised from ibid., 105, where a fuller description of the process is provided.

9. Mary Elizabeth Mullino Moore, *Teaching from the Heart: Theology and Educational Method* (Harrisburg, PA: Trinity Press, 1998).

CPSIA information can be obtained
at www.ICGtesting.com
Printed in the USA
BVOW06s1638150217
476215BV00007BA/53/P